A
**LIBRARY PARTNERS PRESS AWARD
WINNER**

Gail O'Day

POETRY AWARD

The Hopwood Poets Revisited

THE HOPWOOD POETS REVISITED

Eighteen Major Award Winners

EDITED WITH AN INTRODUCTION BY

Donald Beagle

A Library Partners Press Award Winner, 2018

ISBN 978-1618460691

First Edition, Second Printing

Copyright © 2019

Cover art: Meredith Joy Merritt,
"Atmospheric Alchemy;"
[mixed media: nail polish on sandpaper]
Used with permission of the artist.

All rights reserved,
including the right of reproduction,
in whole or in part, in any form.

Produced and Distributed By:

Library Partners Press
ZSR Library
Wake Forest University
1834 Wake Forest Road
Winston-Salem, North Carolina 27106

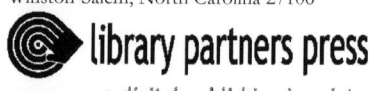

a digital publishing imprint

www.librarypartnerspress.org

Manufactured in the United States of America

This book is

dedicated to

Lily, Lucy, & Will Talbert.

CONTENTS

EDITOR'S INTRODUCTION 1

ROBERT HAYDEN 6
JOHN CIARDI 17
ANNE STEVENSON 28
FRANK O'HARA 35
MARGE PIERCY 47
NANCY WILLARD 54
KEITH WALDROP 67
X. J. KENNEDY 74
PATRICIA HOOPER 83
ROSMARIE WALDROP 88
TOM CLARK 94
LAWRENCE JOSEPH 107
JANE KENYON 113
GARRETT HONGO 132
DONALD BEAGLE 140
LAURA KASISCHKE 155
TUNG-HUI HU 166
DEREK MONG 172

POETS AT MICHIGAN 177

EDITOR'S INTRODUCTION

This book began as a set of Q&A conversations with a select group of living poets who have won Hopwood Awards at the University of Michigan. In reading interviews with poets, I've felt that foundational questions are too often left unasked, and therefore remain unanswered. Understandably, no interviewer wishes to burden a noted author with questions one assumes they may have answered hundreds of times.

But given the remarkable variety of talented poets who have won Hopwood Awards over the decades, my sense was that asking even obvious questions might elicit an interesting variety of replies. So I set my interviewer's ego aside, and began with very basic queries drawn from my experience teaching undergraduate poetry workshops at Duke University in the late 1980's, and (years earlier), at Jackson Community College in Michigan. Having noted that students on these very different campuses tended to ask similar questions of visiting poets, I settled on a handful of standard questions, while adding one or two personalized for each.

But I first posed a question to myself: why hadn't a book with a similar premise ever been published before? Certainly other books related to the Hopwood Awards have appeared — most notably, the fine series of collected lectures delivered by eminent authors at the annual award ceremonies. Walker Percy, for example, delivered the guest lecture when I won in 1977. And 2006 also saw a splendid anthology of poetry and short fiction by Hopwood Award-winning authors assembled from the program's first 75 years.

To quote from the Introduction to that 75th anniversary edition by former Hopwood Program Director Nicholas Delbanco: "Avery Hopwood graduated from the University of Michigan in 1905. He became a successful Broadway playwright, by most accounts the 'richest' of his era, and at his death endowed the prize that bears his name and that of his mother. ….The first awards were offered—and the inaugural lecture delivered—in the academic year 1931-32. No other program in the nation equals it; no other system of institutional reward has recognized so many with so much and for so long. That may sound like hyperbole, but it is researched fact. In the world of higher learning, the Hopwood Awards reign supreme."[1]

As a past winner myself, I obviously agreed. But in re-reading that 75th year anthology, I found myself wanting to learn more about those authors' individual award experiences. Prestigious awards for poetry collections are typically associated with the middle or later periods of a poet's life, when their creative trajectory is established. The Hopwood Award is unusual—and its "major poetry" category for graduate-level collections arguably unique—for being a highly-regarded prize, awarded at a formative and sometimes pivotal period before the poet's career has fully taken shape. And the formative context of those awards, I would suggest, further justified my interest in sending foundational questions with the invitations.

Years passed before I undertook this project, partly because I always assumed someone else (far more qualified, surely) must have such a book already in progress. And there were always the demands of my own writing; ongoing submissions, and the challenging marathon of seeing my first five books (thus far) into publication. Not to ignore my fifty-plus academic research articles, with the attendant complexities of tenure review and approval. But as I first sat down to draft this Introduction, I noted one curious trivia item that may lend an oblique validation to my role in assembling this book. I received my award 39 years after Robert Hayden received his first award, and 39 years before

---

[1] *The Hopwood Awards: 75 Years of Prized Writing*. Edited by Nicholas Delbanco, Andrea Beauchamp, & Michael Barrett. (Ann Arbor: the University of Michigan Press, 2006.) p. 1.

the most recent winners accepted their checks at the podium (as of summer 2016). The reader may thus wish to visualize me sitting in the Buddha's Sukhasana pose, contemplating time present and time past, from my perspective of having experienced an approximate midpoint.

The most obvious editorial challenge was how to structure a book around my personal and email conversations with thirteen living poets, while integrating these with guest essays about the five deceased award winners I most wanted to include (Hayden, Ciardi, O'Hara, Willard, and Kenyon). And a further challenge: how to cultivate this book as an inviting, collegial space that encouraged thoughtful replies and individual reflections without nudging anyone too far toward abstruse theoretics in one direction or cookie-cutter *Wikipedia* digests in another.

Laurence Goldstein's wonderful lead-off essay about his fellow-poet and UM faculty colleague Robert Hayden settled any doubts in my mind about this blended approach. Goldstein's fresh look at Hayden's early poetry, from the poet's personal roots in the Detroit ghetto through his collegiate and faculty years in Ann Arbor, seems to me especially timely. For the other deceased poets, I diverged from the guest essay format only for John Ciardi and Tom Clark. Ciardi's famous columns for *The Saturday Review* were often about poets and poetry, and were typically written in a conversational style. I selected three that seem to fit this book's continuity of content quite well; even to the point of indirectly answering a couple questions asked of the living poets. Tom Clark's remarkable decade-long blog seems to me a freewheeling 21st century counterpoint to Ciardi's columns, and my selections from Clark's Beat-inflected (and copiously illustrated) blog posts quite possibly point the way toward a future where poetry vaults the fault line between the Age of Print and the Digital Age.

To my great delight, Anne Stevenson, X.J. Kennedy, Lawrence Joseph, and Derek Mong also accepted my open invitation to go beyond the

Q&A format to craft their own original essays. But I want to express my sincere gratitude to all the poets and contributors who generously gave their time and attention. I offer a special note of thanks to Rosmarie Waldrop, who somehow found time to send her own reflective replies while coping with her husband Keith's illness. She also conveyed the news that the same would prevent Keith from completing his own contribution. Rosmarie then contacted X. J. (Joe) Kennedy, and (at no prompting from me) Joe responded with his usual generosity, submitting his own superb memoir about his graduate school literary friendship with Keith Waldrop.

I should also mention how poets were chosen for invitations. Since my publisher lacks infinite patience and time, strict selectivity was an inevitable requirement. Here, two factors came into play. On one level, this book echoes, to a significant degree, the selection of poets from that 75th anniversary anthology. Beyond that, it also reflects my publisher's identity as a literary press based in a large academic library. I thus consulted with several library colleagues who generously shared their own expertise in selecting modern poetry collections to support MFA programs at their own universities. Their advice narrowed the range of my invitations a bit further.

As I reviewed the initial list of favorable replies to my invitations, I was delighted by the gender balance that emerged. This reflected, after all, another aspect of the Hopwood Awards' long history: women authors began winning awards nearly from the program's inception in the early 1930's. Sadly, two notable women poets who initially expressed interest—Sarah Messer and Rachel Richardson—ran into deadline constraints on other projects, and are therefore not included. But it seems worth noting that the two longest sections of this book are devoted to Jane Kenyon and Nancy Willard.

Nancy Willard's death, in fact, prompted me to accelerate this project more assertively than I might have anticipated. I was then in the latter stages of assembling the Centennial Edition of Radcliffe Squires' *Selected Poems*. I was just preparing to contact Nancy at Vassar to compare notes on our respective student experiences with Squires as our mutual poetry mentor (albeit years apart), when I received news of her passing. This spurred me to action by emphasizing how many major names associated with Hopwood Awards were already in "that" generation (and older); consequently, how little time likely remained to gather first-person reflections directly from them — or at least (as with Kennedy's essay on Waldrop) indirectly, from their peers. This was dramatized all too poignantly by Tom's Clark's death on August 18, 2018, at age 77, only weeks after he had called to give me permission to "harvest" selected posts from his blog.

With two sections to fill at a late stage, I want to thank Barbara Tierney for updating her 2016 interview with me (originally intended for the library / publishing zine *Against the Grain*); and poet Frances J. Pearce, for redirecting her 2017 interview with me about my experience in editing Radcliffe Squires' *Selected Poems 1950-1985*.

My thanks also go to the University of Michigan's College of Literature, Science & the Arts for generously extending permission for me to publish transcribed excerpts from their three-episode video series, "Poets at Michigan." While the focus of this book is on student poets who have won awards, the LSA video series adds the vital context of those faculty poets who helped guide many of these students. The Hopwoods are not awarded in a vacuum, but within the extraordinary creative envelope of a university that has welcomed a remarkable number of major poets to its faculty, including Robert Frost, W. H. Auden, Theodore Roethke, U. S. Poet-Laureate Donald Hall, Nobel Laureates Czeslaw Milosz and Joseph Brodsky, Macarthur Award-winner Alice Fulton, and others whose names will appear and reappear across these pages.

ROBERT HAYDEN

Hopwood Awards: 1938, 1942

Robert Hayden and *The Black Spear*

By Laurence Goldstein

The Vietnam War was on everyone's mind in 1970 when my wife and I arrived in Ann Arbor to begin my teaching career at the University of Michigan. As it happened, my teaching assistant was a U.S. Army veteran who had just returned from a tour of duty in what he bitterly called "the jungles." During that Fall term I was spending long hours in my seventh floor office in Haven Hall, meeting with freshmen and sophomores, pacing the hallway for exercise and mulling over the day's classes. When I nodded to Robert Hayden sitting in his office he often waved me in for conversation. We talked about our lives, our reading and writing. We talked a lot about the War, and other wars in the nation's history.

Robert and I also chatted about the Apollo 11 moon landing on July 20, 1969. So long ago now, it's easy to forget what an impact that event had on poets and scholars of poetry, how it seemed to affect not only the public consensus on every popular topic, but also the mythology of millennia about the occult relation of humankind and some magical world just beyond our reach. The moon landing had turned the moon into nothing more than "a dead stone in the sky," James Dickey complained. A distant orb hardly worth looking at. Hayden and I kept returning to a strange incident on television, when Walter Cronkite, on the night the Lunar Module *Eagle* landed, invited onto his show an African American man more than a hundred-and-five years old. He could dimly recall being a member of a slave family in the South during the first years of Reconstruction—and now, Cronkite exclaimed, he had lived to a historical moment when Americans were walking on the moon. "Ain't no men on no moon" he spoke back to Cronkite, and when asked to explain, he repeated, more forcefully, *"Ain't no men on no moon!"* Cronkite apologized to his viewers and explained that yes, there were some people who thought that the Apollo 11 mission was just a hoax, a simulation concocted in a TV studio. The old man stared into the camera, a ghost of the 1860s haunting the celebration whirling around him.

In Hayden's poem "Astronauts," published in his last volume, *American Journal*, he calls the pioneers of space travel "heroic antiheroes, / smaller than myth." He spoke to me of the difficulty his generation had in locating and generating myths—stories of almost unimaginable dimensions—and investing them with significance, with the power to move readers to change their minds about issues of racial equality and modern warfare.

Hayden's biographer Pontheolla T. Williams wrote that Hayden's early work, including his Hopwood Award-winning manuscript *The Black Spear*, represented "a fictionalized chronicle of the African American and his acculturation to America."

When Hayden visited my classes to read his poems and answer questions about them he chose works with a long view of the nation's history, reaching back not just to the Civil War but to the first era of slavery: the first Negro poet (Phillis Wheatley), the first Negro casualty in the Boston Massacre (Crispus Attucks):

> I choose him for preamble now
> To covenants of faith we've written here—
> Tall slaveborn Attucks, fugitive,
> Dying in Revolution's square. . .

> He strides into the violent morning
> Of Yankee rage and Hessian gun,
> A giant shouting, Free men, rise
> And strike oppression down.
>
> *from* "Whereas in Freedom's Name. . ."

And he always read to my students "The Ballad of Sue Ellen Westerfield," a dramatic narrative based on his adoptive mother's life on the "tarnished Floating Palaces," the Mississippi riverboats. He read "Belsen: Day of Liberation," and "A Plague of Starlings" about the mass killing of "befouling" black birds on the Fisk campus. Of course he read his signature lyric set in Detroit, "Those Winter Sundays" and several poems on racial antagonism, such as "Runagate, Runagate" about the Underground Railroad, and "Night, Death, Mississippi," about a lynching by the K.K.K. Afterward he worried about bringing such unhappy news from the past to students who faced a grim future in the era of Watergate and the Vietnam War protest marches in Washington D.C. and the murders of Martin Luther King, John and Robert Kennedy, Malcolm X.

Hayden was awarded B.A. and M.A. degrees from the English Department in 1942 and 1944 respectively. He had won two Hopwood Awards, in 1938 and 1942, with only one of the poems from those manuscripts passing into his *Collected Poems* in 1982. "O Daedalus, Fly Away Home," about the myth of Africans' return by physical flight to their original homes (a major motif in Toni Morrison's novel *Song of Solomon*) survived the long passage. All of the other poems from his first book, *Heart-Shape in the Dust* (1940), and his second Hopwood collection, *The Black Spear* (1942), have been omitted all these years. Some of those poems are juvenilia and best left for scholars' eyes only, but a significant number are worthy of reprinting now, since they *will* appear in print in the future, given the nature of digital technology and the accompanying ethic of open access to archival materials.

That is a consummation devoutly to be wished, since the mood of the nation is clearly in tune now with the visions—and they *are* visions, adapted from Biblical sources—that Hayden shaped into different poetic forms throughout what he always called his "'prentice work." The title poem of his Hopwood manuscript, *The Black Spear*, draws together in one voice the rage of John Brown and Harriet Tubman—the subjects of one poem in the volume, and elsewhere a verse play Hayden wrote in the School of Theater featuring the two famous abolitionists in a fictive meeting to plot how to help more slaves fleeing to the North—and the rhetoric of liberation from Frederick Douglass and a small cadre of activist authors. "The Black Spear" was one of the few poems from the Hopwood manuscript that Hayden allowed to be published in an academic journal—*The Michigan Alumnus Quarterly Review*, the parent form of *Michigan Quarterly Review*. The speaker is full of Jeremiah-like anger and warnings of profound changes in the body politic likely to be effected by violent justice. He is possessed by a rage that anticipates "The Ballad of Nat Turner" and the Medusa-inspired vow of vengeance flaming out in "Perseus," one of Hayden's inventive 14-line poems that eschews the harmony of rhyme and the Christian doctrine of forgiveness. "The Black Spear" intones:

> I am the prayer upon whose slow and noiseless stone
> the axe is sharpened, and from the grinding fly
> sparks that shall set slow fire to burning in your walls.
>   *
> I am the match thrown carelessly into dry grass,
> the hidden weapon—the long black spear
> cached under rags and filth and sharpened on a dream.

It is the voice of the renegade slave, of the oppressed and vindictive mass of subjugated, chained, abused figures who seek to unshackle themselves, to change history, to remake America. Hayden was one of these malcontents. "I am native, exile, both," he wrote elsewhere in the manuscript. In the 1960s Hayden was criticized by other black poets for his supposed Uncle Tom concessions to white conventions of poetic decorum and willing assimilation. But in the Hopwood manuscript he had revealed a defiant spirit that sets Black Fire in a historical context.

The spear is ideological, symbolic, very much a literary device. Hayden often told the story of how Stephen Vincent Benét had confessed in his Pulitzer Prize-winning verse epic of the Civil War, *John Brown's Body* (1929), that he lacked the authority to speak about the situation of the Negro:

> O black-skinned epic, epic with the black spear,
> I cannot sing you, having too white a heart,
> And yet, some day, a poet will rise to sing you
> And sing you with such truth and mellowness.

Hayden imagined himself as the chosen voice for that redemptive task. *The Black Spear* is his declaration of independence from the second-rate citizenship impressed on him in his younger years in Detroit. The Hopwood-winning manuscript is filled with historical poems in which black characters speak or are spoken about. They are redemptive poems that envision the body of America as William Blake did in his long poem *America, a Prophecy* (1793) — as a fiery young spirit enraged by abuses the ruling masters have perpetrated on their supposedly inferior servants and slaves. These works are designed to upset and anger the reader by their vivid scenarios of injustice. They belong in a tradition of rousing poems like Paul Laurence Dunbar's "The Haunted Oak" (upon which a black man has been lynched), Robert Lowell's "Christmas Eve Under Hooker's Statue," Gwendolyn Brooks's "The Negro Hero," Allen Tate's "The Swimmers" (also about a lynching), Mari Evans's "Vive Noir," and *many* other protests about the condition of people of color in a land that constantly congratulates itself on its God-given goodness. Hayden shapes another response to that dogma in *The Black Spear*: "there is no hope in Pharaoh's land. . .Go down, Moses, / Way down in Egyptland, / Tell old Pharoah / to let my people // GO. . ."

These passionate poems derive from the Harlem Renaissance, and from the model of poets, and prose writers like Richard Wright, Ann Petry, and Zora Neale Hurston, who tried to reconfigure the literary and racial map of cities and rural homesteads. Hayden edited an anthology for classroom use, *Kaleidoscope,* chronicling the tradition of Negro poetry. He gloried in the flow of African American history and illustrated its currents in poems of incidents, poems about characters, poems that shouted like the preachers' Word and poems that spoke quietly and sadly about failed opportunities to turn historical occasions into radical new forms of communitarian trust and affection. Hayden uses Walt Whitman's book-length sequence about the Civil War, *Drum-Taps*, as a model for his own intentions to set down numerous poems about the war in the same spirit of both sorrow and piety. One can draw a straight line of influence from the poems about the Civil War by Whitman, Herman Melville, and Sidney Lanier to volumes of our own time entirely devoted to the fury and battles of 1860-1865; my favorites are Andrew Hudgins's *After the Lost War* (1988) and Vievee Francis's *Blue-Tail Fly* (2006).

Did Hayden's historical poems, and those of his contemporaries, enable him to write his best-known and most frequently anthologized poems, "Those Winter Sundays" and "The Whipping," about the angry relationships of family members of different generations? Young poets shaping their Hopwood manuscripts are often instructed to compose in opposites: mix hate with love, mix ancestors with the contemporary domestic scene, mix the bardic barbaric yawp with the melodious song and civil discourse. In Hayden's first published volume, *Heart-Shape in the Dust* (1940), this range of lyric statement is on full display. The general topics he would amplify into classic poems in his later work get their first drafts in the style of "People's Poetry," as it was then called, lacking the rhetorical force and vision of *The Black Spear* but laying out the set of emotions, landscapes, and dramatic situations that infuse the great lyrics Hayden composed steadily from the 1940s to 1980, the year of his death.

The Black Spear derives in part from Stephen Vincent Benét's modest apology in *John Brown's Body*, already mentioned. Hayden had wished to add to his manuscript for the Hopwood Awards a long poem connected thematically to the slavery and Civil War lyrics, but he could not complete it to his satisfaction. The poem was "Middle Passage," perhaps his masterpiece. He finally published an early draft in the journal *Phylon* (1945) and also in the hardbound anthology *Cross Section 1945: A Collection of New American Writing*, edited by Edwin Seaver and published by L. B. Fischer Publishing Corp. Despite the obscurity of the Press, the contents include work by Jane Bowles, Gwendolyn Brooks, Norman Rosten, Richard Wright, and other significant rising authors of the mid-1940s. "Middle Passage" adapted the collage structure of T. S. Eliot's *The Waste Land* and Ezra Pound's *Hugh Selwyn Mauberley* for their focus on contemporary social problems, but Hayden's critique of the slave trade exposed the limits of the famous modernists. He emphasized that the horrors of the Middle Passage were directly related to the hypocrisy of Puritan habits of exploitation and greed:

> Standing to America, bringing home
> black gold, black ivory, black seed
>
> Deep in the festering hold thy father lies,
> of his bones New England pews are made,
> those are altar lights that were his eyes

Eliot had borrowed from Shakespeare's *The Tempest* to characterize the waste land of postwar London; Hayden both mimics and critiques Eliot in several places. A racist and anti-Semite, Eliot focused on sexual episodes, adultery and forms of casual coupling, to ground his complaints about the depravity of the modern world. Hayden knew of other, lethal behavior, and documented it. He did not spare native African tribal leaders in the earlier draft of the poem —"our gods false to us, our kings betraying us / scattering us like seeds / to flower stubbornly in alien ground"—but focused almost entirely on the atrocities of the sadists who piloted slave ships with false names like *Jesus, Estrella, Esperanza, Mercy*.

In 1942 the Hopwood Award contest had three judges (for a long time now it has been two judges). The poets who gave Hayden first prize were George Dillon, Marianne Moore, and John Neihardt. Each of them has a significant place in the history of modern American poetry and each had a commitment to drawing into new poems knowledge of the past and familiarity with everyday, esoteric, or native objects.

They recognized the special kind of eloquence in Hayden's technique. Reading the lyrics of *The Black Spear* through the eyes of its judges, one can appreciate how Hayden's command of syntax and lineation, of diction and tone, must have impressed them as worthy of the highest honors.

> Too long, too long have I played banjo songs
> I knew you'd toss me pennies, crusts of bread
> To hear; too long have I essayed
> The roles of beggar and of clown and groveled,
> Singing of welcome-tables in the sky
> Among the ash-heaps for a bone to gnaw,
> A rag to cover me, a tag-end comfort.
>
> But now, in this the hour of decision,
> I smash the banjo's false and hollow music—
> (Gather its fragments, if you will, and lay
> Them with the painted wooden Indian)—

> I pull the time-pocked images of clown
> And beggar, antic groveler, down, and raise
> In their poor stead the image of a man.
>
> *from* "Prologue"

Lines like these constitute a manifesto defiant in its claims for fair treatment in the literary world. These lines and images are the fulfillment of the World War II generation's wrestling with myths and sermons that Hayden made ample use of in the time allotted him to write his major poems. They help to create the traditions visible in much of the first-rate poetry being composed in the twenty-first century by authors of all colors who have learned how to use significant history as well as memorable idioms in crafting successful poems.

The matter of Robert Hayden's presence as a student in Ann Arbor, including his two Hopwood Awards, is narrativized in a novel of 2017 by Paul S. Dimond, *The Belle of Two Arbors*. Dimond has taken advantage of the fact—broadened somewhat in the story line—that Robert Frost, Theodore Roethke, and W. H. Auden inserted themselves into the milieu of creative writers and writing programs at the University of Michigan during the late 1930s and early 1940s. The first mention of Hayden comes from Auden in conversation with the female narrator toward the end of the novel:

[Wystan]. . .told me about a promising young graduate student in his class from Paradise Valley, some "black bottom" section of Detroit, he says. Wystan added, "I think you'd call Robert Hayden a 'Negro' here [in America]. Only glasses as thick as Coke bottle bottoms enable him to see at all, but he's got a way with words and a passion for history and composing." When I asked Wystan whether he was tutoring young Hayden for the Hopwood poetry prize, a wry smile broke out. "I'm trying to help him understand that poetry needs to be about exploring the unknown and writing as you would say at a slant, not political diatribes. . .

Then again, Robert may already be farther along in extracting the dross from his search into slavery and emancipation and composing historical allegories than Isherwood and I were with our political satires." (440)

And a bit later in the novel:

Maybe Auden's protégé, Robert Hayden, had been right: his "Black Spear" poems that won the Major Hopwood prize in 1942 used historical characters and different narrative voices, perspectives, and dialects to reveal how race divided our country. Rabbie hired Hayden as a teaching assistant for the first year writing class and helped the young poet find a job in the library so he could support his wife at home with their baby. (460)

Frederick Glaysher, editor of Hayden's collected volumes of poetry and prose, has published an epic poem, *The Parliament of Poets*, centered on Hayden's transition from the Ann Arbor campus to the heaven of immortal poets, the seat of Apollo on the moon, whence he continues to dispense compelling words of wisdom. Other poets have composed elegies for a poet sorely missed. Hayden enjoyed writing in generic forms like the elegy, as in "Elegies for Paradise Valley" and the abstract "Bone-Flower Elegy," not to mention the large number of character poems that salute the famous departed with biographical rigor: "Homage to the Empress of the Blues" (Bessie Smith), "El-Hajj Malik El-Shabazz" (Malcolm X), "Paul Laurence Dunbar," and many others beginning with "Fire Image" (John Brown) and "Frederick Douglass." And, in *The Black Spear*, a farewell to Beethoven, as if they were, all of them, contemporaries. Well, they *are* contemporaries, ministering as a chorus to the spiritual needs of our strange new republic, now and forever.

***

Manuscript copies of *The Black Spear* are held in the archives of the Hopwood Program, at the University of Michigan; in the Robert Hayden Papers, National Bahá'í Archives, Wilmette, Illinois; and under the administration of the Literary Executor of the Robert Hayden Estate, Frederick Glaysher. The author of this essay is grateful for the help provided by these and other offices and individuals.

***

Laurence Goldstein is Professor Emeritus of English at the University of Michigan and the author of four books of poetry, including *A Room in California*, and several volumes of literary criticism, including most recently *Poetry Los Angeles: Reading the Essential Poems of the City* (2014). Also in this century he has edited *Writing Ann Arbor: A Literary Anthology* and co-edited, with Robert Chrisman, *Robert Hayden: Essays on the Poetry*.

For several decades he was a member of the Hopwood Committee. From 1977 to 2009 he was editor of the University of Michigan's flagship scholarly and creative writing journal, *Michigan Quarterly Review*.

JOHN CIARDI

Hopwood Award: 1939

[**Editor's Note:** John Ciardi attended Tufts University, where he studied with poetry teacher John Holmes. Holmes strongly influenced his student's subsequent career, encouraging Ciardi to apply for admission to the University of Michigan to become a candidate for the Avery Hopwood Award in poetry, which Ciardi subsequently won. That Hopwood Award then facilitated the publication of Ciardi's first collection, *Homeward to America* (1940), and also gained him a fellowship at the Bread Loaf Writers' Conference, of which Ciardi became an influential participant. To quote from John Knott's presentation later in this book: "John Ciardi [was], in his prime, known as a poet and translator, the editor of *The Saturday Review*, a TV and radio personality, and for a number of years, I am told, after WWII, he was simply the most popular poet in the country—the best-known. Like [Arthur] Miller and others, he was drawn to Michigan by the reputation of the Hopwood Awards. Ciardi told me he had borrowed money from his Uncle Max for his tuition, and when Uncle Max asked how he would pay him back, Ciardi said he was going to win a Hopwood Award—and he did."]

Three Columns by John Ciardi from *The Saturday Review*

Sense and Being

It is always a mistake to discuss poetry with a man who insists that it must make sense. It is just possible that sense is what we settle for only when we fall away from the fullest act of being. Who, for example, expects a bridegroom to make sense? We all know him to be too busy with a more enviable condition of being than sense can make. "If I could only live at the pitch that is near madness," writes Richard Eberhart. And adds:

> When everything is as it was in my childhood
> Violent, vivid, and of infinite possibility.

Nonsense, of course. Or nonsense, that is, to the adamantly practical man. But take another look at that man. I see him coming toward me in the shape of a number of large male relatives who assumed the place of my dead father and who were moved by a kindly concern. I had gone to college with the idea of becoming a lawyer, but I got hooked on English courses and kept taking them until I was obviously unemployable. So the sensible avuncular concern of the tribe's senior males. "John," they would say to me, "It's nice to know about all those poetry things, but you gotta be practical." And I would mumble respectful evasions but I would also take a good look at each of them in turn and say to myself, "I wonder what practicality ever did for *him?*"

For the trouble with being sensible is not the sense it does or does not make but the life it never really manages to get to. Sense, as the insistently sensible man practices it, always manages to shut as many doors as it opens. I suspect, in fact, that it shuts far more than it opens. And one of the doors it always shuts, and always with a slam, is poetry.

The slam of that closing door is always the insistence that the poet expound himself in straightforward and logical order. But how can he? The act of writing a poem is never a simple assertion of meaning. It is an act of skill. And an act of skill is precisely one in which the performer must do more things at once than he has time to think about.

On a simple level, riding a bicycle is an act of skill. Let a man try to itemize and account for each of his thousands of balances as he rides his bicycle and he will fall off. The only way to ride it is faster than he can think it. Paradoxically, of course, he must also think it. A rider who forgets he has a bicycle under him is getting ready to fall off. A rider who is aware of the bicycle under him is getting ready to fall off. A rider who is aware of the bicycle under him is forever keeping himself from falling: he senses each imbalance as it develops, and his conditioning produces the counterbalance by reflex. But if he tries to make sense of his reflexive ride, the ride is over.

Let him try to over-rationalize those reflexes, moreover, and he will be in trouble. He might, for example, decide to write a sensible treatise on how to ride a bicycle in good rational order. It might even be a persuasive paper. But were he then to get back on his bicycle and try to ride it according to his own script, nothing could keep him from falling off. It has to be done multiply, by reflex; not monosequentially by theory.

Unlike the bicycle rider, of course, the poet can strike out any part of his ride and any of his falls. There is always that gift of mercy to the artist, and the artist would be a fool not to cherish it. Yet if the poem is to be an achieved act, it can only be brought off as a managed multiplicity, as an act of balancing upon itself, and as one that derives from the poet's whole experience both as a person and as a writer. Every poem he has ever written has a finger in this poem's pie; and everything he ever read, and every sentence he ever parsed, and every man, woman, and child he ever knew, and everywhere he has ever been, and everything he has ever seen, and everything he has ever thought, felt, and – to borrow a coinage from Robert Frost – *thoughtfelt* about any of these conditioning experiences. All these are stored behind the act of writing. Some may be there in neat and conscious storage. Some may be whirling there as some sort of originating chaos. Both the order and the chaos are there as necessary parts of himself, and he must summon both.

The magic of the act of writing is not in its power to make sense, but in its great power to quicken and summon this memorial mass of the self. As the poem begins to buzz, endless possibilities offer themselves; possibilities that were not there a word, a phrase, an image, a rhyme, or a cadence ago.

But these possibilities can only exist as a sort of side vision. Turn on them the full rational-cognitive stare of the logician as biomechanic, and they disappear. For one can no more demand them than he can demand the sequences of a dream. One of the blindnesses of the man of insistent sense follows directly from the fact that what he insists on is that full rational-cognitive stare. Instantly, then his side vision is lost.

The poet knows better. He knows that language, rhyme, image, rhythm, and form are means of knowledge and that they are the means of a knowledge that cannot be acquired scientifically, or mechanically, or, in general, "sensibly" as the insistently sensible man means the word.

The human race has been shaping language from its earliest beginning, and language has been shaping the human race. Whatever else a man is, he is bound to be a product of his own use of language. By some process at least remotely related to natural evolution, moreover, language has adapted itself to man's needs. Let a man teach himself, not to make statements, but to hearken to his own fullest language, and the language will infallibly inform him as he works to bring it to form. How can he know what the language will say next? – he has to wait for the language to say it to him.

What he is waiting for is his act of language. Like the dream that most tells him who he is, does not say things; it takes place. The important difference between the dream and the poem is that he has no control over the dream. He has to let it happen. And the poem he must *make* happen.

Of what sort of knowledge? Imagine yourself as having stood by Shakespeare's deathbed watching his eyes. You might then find yourself in the context that might answer: it is the knowledge of everything that went out when those eyes closed.

It is the sort of knowledge no man can take by assault. It is the sum of what he learns by living his life in his mind's fullest waking. And that order of living, as I believe I have learned, can be won to only when the poet – or any other artist – has given himself in trust to his medium, because he knows his medium is a sentient and an active thing, and that wherever it takes him will be toward life.
September 19, 1964

Poetry and Luck

In art, good luck happens only to those who have earned it. The minimum requirement for a good poem, I have argued in the past, is a miracle. It now occurs to me that I was simply restating Keats' thought that poetry should surprise with "a fine excess." The poem has to turn out better than anyone, the poet included, could have foreseen that it would, or could have expected it to. That is the miracle: the poem must in some way outrun what seemed possible. It must somehow be struck by lightning. As, say, Emily Dickinson was when she set out to describe her innate revulsion at the sight of a snake and found herself saying that she never came upon one

> Without a tighter breathing
> And Zero at the bone.

Think of the endless ways in which that line might have been nothing. An unlucky, unmiraculous, unlightning-struck poet might have written "And a shudder deep inside," or "And a shiver of the spine," or "And a tingle of revulsion." Had that same poet let those lines stand he would, of course, have been guilty of that esthetic immorality that tolerates shoddy as real stuff. But no matter how firm his refusal to stock bad goods, only a poet moved by lucky lightning could have struck from the page the ominous scraping *zizz* of that Zero.

Nothing but luck can do, but that luck is not free; the lightning must be worked for.

That work begins with the act of meaning the poem hard enough to reject such spineless bad lines as I have improvised as alternates, in refusing to settle for anything but true lightning. But it only begins there.

Having declared against all that is not lightning, how do the good poets get to the lightning itself, or it to them? For if to be struck by such blessed lightning is a piece of luck, it is a kind of luck that happens over and over to some people, and never to others. Some poets obviously know how to woo that lightning. It is in the wooing, in their devotion to the discipline of love, that they earn their luck.

Think of it in terms of a perhaps entirely frivolous figure. The good poet is a student of lightning. He keeps weather charts and he keeps them constantly to hand. He develops a feel for where the thunderheads are. He also keeps some sort of emotional helicopter ready. As soon as he spots a thunderstorm he is on his way to it. There he instinctively places himself under the tallest tree, makes sure he is soaking wet and standing in a puddle, wraps himself in chains for good measure, and holds up a lightning rod.

He won't catch the lightning every time. Luck cannot always be with him. But he is ready for whatever luck will come. He has earned it. And he must inevitably have more luck than the dry and stormless souls that live in Faraday cages.

A Faraday cage, in case you were asleep that day in first-year physics, is roughly speaking, an enclosure shielded from outside electrical forces. An automobile is more or less a Faraday cage, unless it is grounded by a chain, as fuel trucks are. A mental Faraday cage is an emotional inclosure shielded from the storm of ideas. It will get you from womb to tomb dry and unshocked – unless the road gives out or you wreck it. But it runs to one side of poetry.

The good poet earns his luck by living closer to the weather.

But if there is no esthetic luck without devotion, it is still in fact luck, and devotion alone will not bring the lightning down. If all men are created equal as a political premise, what follows their creation spreads them out with considerable differences between them. How many men are created as equal as, say, Robert Frost?

There has to be not only devotion and risk but a talent for the weather. In poetry, that weather talent is locked into the poet's feel for words and images and rhythms and forms as living systems of things. He generates meaning – enduring and dramatic enactments of what it means to be a self-registering personality in a self-consuming body. But it is not meaning as such he pursues. He is after the *thingness* of the word, the image, the rhythm, and the form. The *thingness* is his weather. He has no need to mean it: he lives it. He does not tell a poem: he experiences it. He experiences himself into it. It comes to him as a cloud and he enters it, not knowing where he will come out, but certain that whatever essential lightning there may be in his life has to be in that cloud or another like it. And certain, too, that when the lightning does strike – if it does strike – he will know that it is in fact lightning, and not "a shudder deep inside," nor "a shiver of the spine," nor "a tingle of revulsion."

That is the other thing about lightning: one has to learn to accept no substitutes. But how? How can one be sure that he hasn't been settling for static electricity, which his nerves have been registering as lightning? I suspect one never ultimately knows. Perhaps it is more nearly a matter of praying for rather than knowing. I have known men I surely believe to be bad poets who were yet entirely and prayerfully convinced that they were toward the lightning. So perhaps do all men delude themselves. It is always possible to fail. But one tries at least to fail into the weather.

If there is any luck to be had, that's where it is.
October 21, 1961

On Form as a Language

The more I hear teachers talk about the meaning of poetry (by which they always seem to mean paraphrasable content), the more I suspect them of talking that way because they never learned how to talk about form. I do not mean to imply that poetry has no meaning. Meaning in poetry is inevitable but secondary – still assuming, that is, that by "meaning" one means "paraphrasable content."
If, however, "meaning" is taken to mean the "intention" of a poem, then let it be added that the meaning is never in the subject content but always and only in the way that content is fused into form. Form is always first.

For the poem is not a statement but a verbal artifact. It exists as a painting or a piece of sculpture or a piece of music exists. It is a wrought entity. It is not simply a sequence of words and phrases. It has *thingness*. It exists as a form. The act of the writing is the act of reaching for the completion of whatever form offers itself. Nor is the poet opposed to meaning in the act of reaching. Rather, form is the language in which he means. The poem is finished, so to speak, when the form has signaled itself to a close.

There is nothing mysterious about the way a poetic form signals itself to a close; every reader knows something about it. He has at least noticed that when Shakespeare writes a soliloquy in blank verse, he is likely to end it with one or two rhymed couplets. The rhyme serves as the closing bell. The listener hears it and knows the passage has been brought to rest.

It is, to be sure, a bit more complicated than that. The rhythm of the saying, the sound of it, the emotional enlargement of the dramatic situation, and the paraphrasable content of the passage must all be manipulated in such a way that they come to rest together in those final chimes. But even a gross simplification of the case is enough to suggest one general rule: *form tends to conclude itself by some increase in formality*.

And the rule so derived from Shakespeare's use of blank verse will apply as readily to poetry written in other conventions. If the poet is writing in rhymed couplets, for example, the addition of one more couplet will not in itself signal the passage to an end, but some other increase in formality can do so. Alexander Pope is likely to conclude his paragraphs of rhymed couplets with a particularly good pointed parallelism, with a balanced antithesis, with some other grammatical or rhetorical formality, with a particular management of the sound and stress of the voice, or with some combination of these.

Just as certainly, a series of double rhymes can be rounded home on a final chord of triple rhymes. And many poets have given the closing signal to a sequence of iambic pentameter couplets by ringing in a final alexandrine. An alexandrine is technically no more than an iambic hexameter, but when it is used in this way it tends to be further characterized by a rather formal pause in the middle with the rhythm and grammar (or both) of the last three feet repeating or complementing that of the first three.

Pope, I must note, thought badly of alexandrines. The famous passage of "An Essay on Criticism" in which he ticks off, while imitating, the bad habits of poetasters concludes:

> Then, at the last and only couplet fraught
> With some unmeaning thing they call a thought,
> A nameless Alexandrine ends the song,
> That, like a wounded snake, drags its slow length along.

English teachers, however, ought not to assume that the whole law has been spoken in a simple deft lampoon. The alexandrines Pope had in mind may have been pedestrian, but the need for them was formal, and there is nothing to keep a good poet from writing such alexandrines to good effect. They remain a still usable, though minor, mechanical resource.

Another sort of formal completion is the one I think of as *thematic*. It consists of getting two different tonalities going in a poem to rest by blending the two into one. Marianne Moore's "Nevertheless" is a particularly firm example of this sort of form. The poem begins (and the title must be read as part of the saying):

> you've seen a strawberry
>   that's had a struggle; yet
>   was, where the fragments met
>
> a hedgehog or a star-
>   fish for the multitude
>   of seeds.

The poem continues in this tone for six stanzas, reveling in minutely observed details of such particularities as prickly pears and the "leaves of *kok-saghyz*-stalks" (*kok-saghyz* is a species of dandelion from the roots of which the Russian make rubber, the *WNW* spells it without the *h*). Then, between the seventh and the either stanzas, a new tone enters:

> as carrots form mandrakes
> > or a ram's-horn root some-
> > > times. Victory won't come
> to me unless I go to it;

Thereafter the poem returns to the first tone until the last two stanzas, which read:

> The weak overcomes its
> > menace, the strong over-
> > > comes itself. What is there
> like fortitude! What sap
> > went through that little thread
> to make the cherry red!

What has happened? Let me suggest that the reader can readily enough find out for himself either from these fragments or from the total poem (it may be found in the *Collected Poems*, published by Macmillan).

Let him begin by calling that first tone "botanical observations" and the second "moral statements." Then let him go through the poem underlining every "botanical observation" in blue and every "moral statement" in red.

My hope is that by the time he finds himself underlining the last two and a half lines in purple, he will have discovered for himself something about the way in which form is its own language.

October 31, 1964

ANNE STEVENSON

Hopwood Awards: 1951, 1952, 1954

Letter to Donald Beagle

Dear Don,

Having no family obligations this year, I have set aside these dark days of the solstice to think about your questions relating to the Major Hopwood Prize I won as a Senior at the University of Michigan as long ago as 1954. I'm pretty sure that the day I walked into the Reception Office of Martha Cook and found a note in my pigeonhole congratulating me on having won a Hopwood Prize was the happiest day of my undergraduate life. I remember uttering a whoop of delight and rushing up the stairs to my roommate, telling everyone I met on the way of my triumph. And though I don't remember having re-read my prize-winning poems when I returned as a graduate student to Ann Arbor in 1960, or indeed when I spent six months there as a Rackham fellow in 1994, I kept copies of my undergraduate dance drama, *The Silver Heron,* and the libretto I wrote for a short opera, *Adam & Eve & and the Devil* (music by a student friend, Karl Magnusson) until 1998, when I gave all my college manuscripts, together with those of my Hopwood poems to the Cambridge University Library in England. I have always written from the same musical impulse and from a need to explore, explain and express facets of my own experience. The poems I submitted to the Hopwood judges were written from the same inexplicable need that still (though more rarely) surprises me today, a kind of hunger to find enduring words and language-rhythms for feelings that are usually suppressed or filed down or ignored by automatic habits of thinking.

The immediate effect of that major award was to pay for my flight to Cambridge, England, where, having failed to get a Fulbright fellowship to Italy to study the connection between poetry and music in opera libretti, I decided to marry a Cambridge University Rugby player instead and live happily ever after in the image of my mother while nevertheless becoming the poet my Hopwood Prize had convinced me I just might be. It never occurred to me that a conflict could arise between family love and the complete dedication to the arts that I had experienced at Michigan. But, of course, like many thousands of women graduates at the time – and perhaps especially those like Sylvia Plath and myself who married Englishmen – any strong ambition to write and publish ran straight into a barrier of social expectations that tied a wife to her husband's career and persuaded her to abandon her own. Young, free and childless in London and Cambridge in the mid 1950s, it never occurred to me that the very fact that I was the American wife of an *ingénue* business consultant who had nothing to do with the arts debarred me from the exclusive, very competitive, merciless world of professional literature, even when poems of mine were accepted by literary journals. A Major Hopwood Award meant nothing to the editors of the *TLS*, or indeed, of *The New Yorker*. Moving with my husband from job to job and city to city in England and Ireland before settling in the American South meant I made few connections of my own, and later, of course, I discovered that childbearing and child-raising, no matter how much you love your child, blunts the mind and the imagination. Days are filled with tedious chores; nights are often sleepless. That Hopwood triumph faded year by year into an impossible ideal until there came a point when I had to confess, both to myself and to my puzzled English husband, that I had taken a wrong turning, that to avoid breakdown I needed to return to an environment where poetry thrives. In short, I broke away from that marriage on purely selfish grounds and went 'home' to Ann Arbor where my life in poetry began again in 1960 under the tutelage of Donald Hall and as a teaching assistant to Radcliffe Squires.

You ask me to name the poets who most affected the formative process in my work. Hall and Squires were in their different ways inspiring, and they certainly introduced me to influential mid-century contemporaries. Hall led his students into a world of startling new poetry with informed readings of Wallace Stevens, Robert Lowell, Randall Jarrell, Marianne Moore and to me, most importantly Elizabeth Bishop, on whose work he found me a commission to write the first full-length study for Twayne's United States Authors Series. Squires, when I was his assistant, was writing on Robert Frost, an early and lasting favourite of mine, many of whose poems I had "learned by heart" in high school. But my deepest debt, prior to any university influences, was surely to my father, whose family readings of Shakespeare, the Romantic poets and the English Victorians when I was a child had saturated my ear before I was well aware that iambic pentameter and variations thereof was the metrical basis of English verse. As a philosopher and teacher, musician and superb reader, my father, Charles Stevenson, was probably the source both of the unsettled questioning that runs through many of my poems and equally of their rhythmic certainty. The rhythmic certainty derived, I'm sure, from his readings of Yeats; the philosophical skepticism from his own debt to David Hume. From my mother, Louise Stevenson, I inherited a life-long devotion to the prose of Jane Austen, whose six novels I still read and re-read whenever in need of spiritual consolation. Had I been given a choice, I would have written novels. But my gifts were neither sufficiently expansive nor free of rhythmic restrictions for prose. It was as much the music of poetry as the meaning that lured me into verse.

Your third question, Don, divides into three parts, the second of which relates to the "transatlantic aspect" of my life and work. It has taken me the better part of a lifetime to understand my attraction, even as a small child, to England, English literature and Englishness. The fact that I had been born in England, that my Ohio-born parents had begun life together in Cambridge and passed on their passion for English literature to me, that in New Haven during the War we adopted two English girls whose brother became a sort of half brother to my sister and myself—all these factors played on my imagination, creating a fantasy that I for years embroidered into a fictional self that I see now was quite distinct from the ambitious American student-musician-poet I actually was. Much as I robustly believed in the life I led and enjoyed at Michigan, I still cast myself secretly as the heroine of stories I had been embroidering in my imagination since the age of twelve. It was harmless, I thought, like indulging a dream, to pretend I was a female re-incarnation of John Keats, or about to marry Mr. Darcy, or to enrich English literature in the future with my wonderful fiction. It wasn't until I had married and lived for three of four years in bombed, shabby, rationed post war London that the dream dispersed and shattered. I returned with my little girl to the USA to confront some very bleak months before and after my mother died, realizing with poignant clarity that my childish English escape-fantasies had nothing to do with poetry. From now on, I told myself, I will follow the footprints of Yeats, Frost, Eliot, and W.H. Auden; I will learn from studying Elizabeth Bishop, stop being envious of Sylvia Plath, and in my own poems, write, as far as I can, the truth of what happens.

As it turns out, I have spent far more of my life in England, Scotland and Wales than in the United States, but this is because my personal tastes and a sequence of life-determining choices repeatedly pulled me away from what might have been an academic career in poetry. I have always felt that a poet writes better from a marginal, uncommitted position outside any academic career structure, opposing an intuitive self-perception to the nagging egotism that encourages him or her to care too much about making a name and a reputation. I will come back to this later, when I attempt to answer your sixth question relating to the place of a working poet in modern academia.

I suppose that the conviction I acquired in the early sixties that writing poetry always entails a straight, sometimes tragic, sometimes comic look at reality, explains why I never have felt attached to any contemporary school or group of poets. The long, still surviving Anglo-American tradition of lyrical and dramatic verse that had somehow been bred into my bones was school enough. I have been aware, of course, of the successive waves of poetic fashion as they succeeded each other in my lifetime: women-poets, confessionals, the Beats, the Black Mountain poets, the post-modernists etc. But here Elizabeth Bishop, who would have nothing to do with theories, became my mentor. A poem is neither interesting nor moving if it is not individual and within its chosen pattern, original, and so, to some degree subversive. Whatever form it takes, there is always that "wildness whereof it is made" that Robert Frost identified long before the Beats came along. Yes, I am sympathetic with today's so-called Formalists, although I am wary of cliché verse forms and doggerel. The more formal a poem's pattern, the more original its language, word affinities and ideas have to be.

Poetry readings? I confess I am usually happier giving them than listening to them, but this is chiefly because I have become so deaf over the years that I wear two hearing aids, one a cochlear implant, so any public lecture or reading is a trial to me. If a poet reads well, however, and his or her poems have conviction and are worth hearing, I usually manage to hear them. An enduring test for new poems, even now, is how well they sound when read aloud or recited.

To return to your sixth and last question: "Do you see modern academia in general as a good professional base for working poets?" Having learned so much from the teaching and friendship of Donald Hall and Radcliffe Squires in the early 1960s, I am embarrassed to confess that for *working poets* I fear that a university career teaching or majoring in Creative Writing – unless one is well acquainted with the literature of the past before confronting the theories of the present – can turn into a destructive trap. For although you can teach students how to write clearly, to read sensitively and to follow metrical rules, there seems to me no way to teach 'creativity', which is a gift bestowed on rare individuals and needs to be worked on independently, unsparingly and constantly but not subjected to any standard formulas of excellence. Universities are invaluable purveyors of literary criticism, of course, and preservers as well as promoters of all the arts. Like all save very popular writers through the ages, poets have needed patrons. Where emperors, kings, courts and wealthy patrons have supported artists in the past, universities now supply necessary jobs. I would go so far as to say that in Britain and America the universities, together with a number of intelligent, well written journals and newspapers, are today the only reliable protectors of artistic excellence, since the Internet, having remodeled time and space in its own image, has created a dangerous democracy of everybody and everything that makes discrimination between good, bad and indifferent art difficult to defend in populist terms.

When you ask, "Do you feel the role of the poet in the academy has had any discernible impact – positive or negative – upon poetry in general in the US and the UK?" I would probably say, given the enormous increase in the number of poems being written every day in English now (hundreds, thousands?), that there has been proportionally a leveling down of quality. A great deal of not bad, even publishable poetry exists, but very little of it would even pretend to be major or lasting. There are also many good serious poets writing now; I know and admire many personally and profit from corresponding with them. But again, I hesitate to call any of them 'great'. And there is always, of course, the *avant garde*, the daring, self-conscious innovators who call attention to themselves by throwing away tradition and founding poetry anew in corners of the more sophisticated periodicals. But mainly, university poetry – and indeed, community poetry – thrives as a social asset, and as thousands of well-meaning and naturally self-interested people, young and old, enjoy writing and exchanging their poems, it would be churlish to complain. We can only be grateful that writing poetry has become a common pursuit enjoyed by many people who, ambitious or not, have at least found a way to affirm their humanity independently of the insult done to it by the language of Twitter and Facebook. Whether the world of the future will have time for poetry, or indeed, amateur (in the right sense) painting and classical music, depends on how much strength mere human beings can muster to oppose the gods of automation, instant communication and political violence they have recently and so terribly creatively brought into being.

Anne Stevenson
1st January 2018

FRANK O'HARA

Hopwood Award: 1951

"Introduction" [excerpt]

From "Introduction," by Bill Berkson, in: Frank O'Hara, *Poems Retrieved*. Edited by Donald Allen. (San Francisco: City Lights / Grey Fox, c2013).

"….The breadth of what Frank O'Hara took to be poetry is reflected in the many kinds of poems he wrote. The quick release from riveted (and riveting) attentiveness to direct response being his mission and métier, the rate of response, as well as the wide net cast by his attentions throughout, is extraordinary, as if the world would stop without his continually remarking on its activities. Turning the pages of any of his collections, you wonder what he didn't turn his hand to, what variety of poem he left untried or didn't, in some cases, as if in passing, anticipate.

> I see my vices
> lying like abandoned works of art
> which I created so eagerly
> to be worldly and modern
> and with it

About Frank O'Hara's earliest writings John Ciardi, whose workshops O'Hara took at Harvard, recalls: 'He showed his brilliance rather than his feelings. That was a point I often made in talking about his writing. I think, in fact, it was when he used his brilliance to convey rather than to hide behind that he found his power.' What John Ashbery calls O'Hara's 'period of testing' continued for some time beyond his student years, and, sensibly enough, a good three-quarters of *Poems Retrieved* is taken up with poems dating from that time (roughly 1950–1954), after which anything he wrote was less prone to fall short of the mark. As late as 1952 in New York, he is still signing poems with his Hopwood Award pen name 'Arnold Cage.'....Part of O'Hara's youthful testing was his willingness to try out, beside a slew of poetic personae, any available forms and genres: accordingly, among the poems here are epigrams (many of those spot-on), eclogues, calligrams, sestinas, sonnets, quatrains and tercets and rhymed couplets, birthday poems and envois, poems in prose, one-liners and lines of great mystery and beauty ("Sentimentality, aren't you sunset?"...). There are fragments that stay fragments and have a kind of inviolable strength, like bits of antique parchment..."

[This excerpt of 330 words from Berkson's "Introduction," including 23 words from a poem by O'Hara, is reproduced here under provision of Academic Fair Use].

[**Editor's Note**: The following is excerpted from Charles Altieri's 1973 essay, "The Significance of Frank O'Hara." as published in *The Iowa Review* 4.1 (1973): 90-104. I want to extend my sincere thanks to Dr. Altieri for his permission to republish this excerpt from his essay. I encourage interested readers to peruse the original article in its entirety. The decision to include an excerpted version is based only on editorial constraints, and should in no way be interpreted as a judgment that this excerpt is a worthy substitute for the whole.]

The Significance of Frank O'Hara

By Charles Altieri

"...O'Hara's life provides fictions both more superficial and more interesting than pure fantasy or artifice. The poet keeps his story alive by a loving fidelity to the specific facts and qualities of his daily experience seen for themselves and not as the building blocks of larger, more significant wholes traditionally called poems:

> 'I am mainly preoccupied with the world as I experience it, and at times when I would rather be dead the thought that I could never write another poem has so far stopped me. . . . What is happening to me, allowing for lies and exaggerations which I try to avoid, goes into my poems. I don't think my experiences are clarified or made beautiful for myself or anyone else,. . . It may be that poetry makes life's nebulous events tangible to me and restores their detail; or conversely, that poetry brings forth the intangible quality of incidents which are all too concrete and circumstantial.' (CP, 500)

It is in this context of life continually providing materials for the story that we must understand O'Hara's love affair with New York City (cf. "Steps," CP, 370-71). For the city is a continual source of interesting and engaging details. Moreover, the city is a perfect metaphor for O'Hara's sense of the value in these details. Presence in the city is antithetical to presence in nature. City details after all have neither meaning, hierarchy nor purpose not created absolutely by man. And more important, the city is committed to perpetual change; there are no enduring seasonal motifs or patterns of duration underlying and sustaining the multiplicity of city phenomena. They exist completely in the moment. And they exist superficially. In the city, as in O'Hara's ontology, interesting and engaging details are continually becoming present. Yet not only do these momentary apparitions promise no underlying significance or meanings to be interpreted, they actually resist any attempt on our part to know them better. City life offers a series of phenomena to notice, perhaps to play with in one's own psyche, but very rarely do these phenomena inspire or welcome any attempt to participate in their lives.

O'Hara's analogue for the specific form of presence manifested by the city is his way of naming. His texture of proper names gives each person and detail an identity, but in no way do the names help the reader understand anything about what has been named. To know a lunch counter is called Juliet's Corner or a person O'Hara expects to meet is named Norman is rather a reminder for the reader that the specific details of another's life can appear only as momentary fragments, insisting through their particularity on his alienation from any inner reality they might possess. What makes O'Hara so interesting a poet is his sense at once of the necessity for story, of its superficiality, and of the pain potentially lurking in every moment. The dialectic between presence and alienation we find in his use of names is more strikingly evident in the larger rhythms of his work. Coexisting with O'Hara's evident joy in a kaleidoscopic rush of details and encounters are frequent perceptions of a lurking anxiety ready to seize him if the flow of events should give it a moment's foothold:

> I ducked out of sight behind the saw-mill
> nobody saw me because of the falls and the gates the sluice the
>   tourist boats
> the children were trailing their fingers in the water
> and the swans, regal and smarty, were nipping their "little"
>   fingers
> I heard one swan remark "That was a good nip
> though they are not as interesting as sausages" and another
> reply "Nor as tasty as those peanuts we got away from the
>   elephant that time"
> but I didn't really care for conversation that day
> I wanted to be alone
> which is why I went to the mill in the first place
> now I am alone and hate it
> I don't want to just make boards for the rest of my life
> I'm distressed
> the water is very beautiful but you can't go into it

because of the gunk
and the dog is always rolling over, I like dogs on their 'little"
    feet
I think I may scamper off to Winnipeg to see Raymond
but what'll happen to the mill
I see the cobwebs collecting already
and later those other webs, those awful predatory webs
if I stay right here I will eventually get into the newspapers
like Robert Frost
willow trees, willow trees they remind me of Desdemona
I'm so damned literary and at the same time the waters rushing
    past remind me of
                                        nothing

I'm so damned empty
what is all this vessel shit anyway
we are all rushing down the River Happy Times
ducking poling bumping sinking and swimming
and we arrive at the beach
the chaff is sand
alone as a tree bumping another tree in a storm
that's not really being alone, is it, signed The Saw
(CP, 428-429)

To be "alone" is also to be all one, but again like city life O'Hara has only the unity of mad process trying to make up in motion what it lacks in meaning. The self threatens always to dissipate into the surfaces it contemplates, to become merely a "skein of lust" (CP, 403) unwinding in time. Yet one need only recognize the dangers to overcome them, to reaffirm his commitment and love of the processes he's engaged in: one must maintain, he tells us in his essay on Nakian, "a kind of despairing sensual delight" by achieving "a relation with physical truth that is both stoic and sybaritic."[2] Notice how in the poem I've quoted, O'Hara never dwells on the problems but keeps turning instead to the details of the scene or his own fantasies of future possibilities. "Naphtha" offers an even better example of a conclusion nicely capturing both the underlying sterility of his experience and the rich union of stoic and sybaritic he makes of it:

> how are you feeling in ancient September
> I am feeling like a truck on a wet highway
> how can you
> you were made in the image of god
> I was not
> I was made in the image of a sissy truck-driver
> and Jean Dubuffet painting his cows
> "with a likeness burst in the memory"
> apart from love (don't say it)
> I am ashamed of my century
> for being so entertaining
> but I have to smile
>
> (CP, 338)

He "has" to smile because he has no alternative, but also because his and his century's absurd situation are genuinely entertaining. O'Hara has to smile, not to laugh, and in that small difference we can realize the distance between his genuinely sybaritic stoicism and the less humane anguish of the black humorist.....

The poet illustrates and exemplifies modes of engaging whatever experiences a person might have, and his work becomes testament to

---

[2] Quoted in Richard Howard's fine essay on O'Hara in *Alone With America* (New York: Atheneum, 1971), p. 403.

the kind of effects these attitudes might have.³ This sense that poetry is moral through the attitudes it embodies permeates contemporary poetry, and O'Hara is an influential example of both a specific strategy and the general framework supporting such an emphasis: think for example of poets like Gary Snyder, Allen Ginsberg, Bly and W. S. Merwin, who seek to embody modes of consciousness which one can or must inhabit to intuit moral truths; or consider others like John Logan, Bill Knott, David Ignatow and John Ashbery (O'Hara's close friend whose ironic and disembodied voice suggests a mode of living almost exactly opposite O'Hara's, though the two share the same ontology) whose attitudes are more directly moral, more concerned with ways of acting in relation to suffering and to other people, than they are with leading us to ontological truths. What all share, though, is a tendency to expand traditional lyric modes so that they become existential strategies.

Lyric poetry has always had as its primary function the invention and testing of attitudes toward experience, and persona was a primary critical category for critics of the fifties. But within the tradition attitude was always supplementary to the moral qualities of the experience itself. Thus critics and poets could conceive persona ironically and contemplate the gap between ideal modes of response suggested by the experience and the specific moral or intellectual failures of the specific voice in the poem. Contemporary poets cannot afford to be ironic about their persona because they cannot trust, either in the poem or in reality, that the experience itself provides norms for judging the response. Rather only the response itself — its appeal for the reader and the possibilities it offers for keeping him open to the reality of his own experiences — can be the measure of the poet's moral value.

---

[3] This is precisely what Robert Motherwell does in O'Hara's collection of his work and his reflections, *Robert Motherwell* (New York: The Museum of Modern Art, 1965), p. 53.

O'Hara's specific attitude is also very influential, not only to those New York poets who continue in the pop art tradition but to others more taken by his humility and affirmative skepticism. The qualities of skepticism and humility in fact often go hand in hand, for it is always tempting, if not always possible, to extend one's skepticism about external values to skepticism about the self. And O'Hara's poetry does just that: one so aware of the arbitrary creativity he requires to keep the present vital is not apt to take either himself, his poetry, or his world view as possible salvation for everyone. So O'Hara presents us with demystified views of both the reconciliation of opposites and the poetic image….

Paul Carroll is the first critic I know to claim a really influential role in contemporary poetry for O'Hara. My argument complements and extends his, which deals primarily with the aesthetic aspects of the themes of domesticity and the process of continual creation. O'Hara's influence, he says, stems from three related factors in his work. He makes clear for poets how the dada and expressionist doctrines of creation can work for them, for his poems continually insist that they are not representations of reality but the enactment by the artist of certain attitudes and choices within that reality. Consequently there are no canonical or privileged subjects for poetry: "Anything, literally, can exist in a poem; and anything can exist in whatever way the poet chooses." O'Hara then shows how the poet need no longer feel committed to organic unity as a principle of poetic construction. His details need not be chosen because they enhance a specific lyric point or attitude; the objects chosen can embody the multiple facets of experience, only some of which might be essential to the lyric feeling. This anti organicist aesthetic Carroll defines as the aesthetic of the "impure poem."[4] The idea of the "impure poem" is both helpful and dangerous. It is helpful in so much as it calls our attention to the materials and attitudes the contemporaries try to give poetic

---

[4] Paul Carroll. *The Poem In Its Skin* (Chicago: Follett, 1968), 157-165; quote p. 163.

expression, but it oversimplifies the texture of relationships in the best poems using such materials. The organic poem need not be the single-minded evocation of simple emotions; "organic" simply means that all the aesthetic choices contribute to the complex effect of the poem. It is true that many of O'Hara's poems do not aim at single lyric effects but focus instead, like Duchamp's urinal and Warhol's Campbell's soup cans, on celebrating the powers of artistic choice and thus reminding us of the simple levels at which value experience continually takes place. But O'Hara's best lyrics employ details both as specific references to an impure, discontinuous texture of experience and as carefully related elements in a complex lyric feeling. "The Day Lady Died" is Carroll's example of the archetypal impure poem; but that poem to me is one of the finest examples of the rich poetic possibilities in the domestic lyric O'Hara encouraged. The poem not only captures the vitality of pre-reflective experience but arranges that experience so it participates in and evokes for consciousness a complex, satisfying and relatively traditional lyric emotion:

> It is 12:20 in New York a Friday
> three days after Bastille day, yes
> it is 1959 and I go get a shoeshine
> because I will get off the 4:19 in Easthampton
> at 7:15 and then go straight to dinner
> and I don't know the people who will feed me
>
> I walk up the muggy street beginning to sun
> and have a hamburger and a malted and buy
> an ugly NEW WORLD WRITING to see what the poets
> in Ghana are doing these days
> I go on to the bank
> and Miss Stillwagon (first name Linda I once heard)
> doesn't even look up my balance for once in her life
> and in the GOLDEN GRIFFIN I get a little Verlaine
> for Patsy with drawings by Bonnard although I do
> think of Hesiod, trans. Richmond Lattimore or

> Brendan Behan's new play or Le Balcon or Les Negres
> of Genet, but I don't, I stick with Verlaine
> after practically going to sleep with quandariness
>
> and for Mike I just stroll into the PARK LANE
> Liquor Store and ask for a bottle of Strega and
> then I go back where I came from to 6th Avenue
> and the tobacconist in the Ziegfeld Theatre and
> casually ask for a carton of Gauloises and a carton
> of Picayunes, and a NEW YORK POST with her face on it
> and I am sweating a lot by now and thinking of
> leaning on the John door in the 5 SPOT
> while she whispered a song along the keyboard
> to Mal Waldron and everyone and I stopped breathing
> (CP, 325)

One way of seeing how the poem is impure, Carroll suggests, is to recognize that twenty lines are devoted to the casual events of O'Hara's day and only four to the ostensive subject of the poem. He goes on, though, to offer two insights which help explain how the artist's apparently free creative selection of details really creates a single complex lyric emotion:

> "I wonder how touching that beautiful final memory . . . would be if O'Hara had preceded it with emotional tributes and 'props' customary in most traditional elegies. . . . In another sense, 'The Day Lady Died' isn't about Billie Holliday at all. It is about the common but sobering feeling that life continues on its bumbling way despite the tragic death of an important artist or some loved one."[5]

---

[5] Carroll, p. 160.

But it is not only the general configuration of details, the contrast between bumbling life and the suddenness of death which unifies the poem. The actual particulars by which the poem captures the vitality of life at the same time constantly call attention to their own contingency and perpetual hovering on the brink of disconnection.

O'Hara has plans for dinner but doesn't know the people who will feed him; he is divorced in space and attitude from the Ghana poets, in time and habit from the writers mentioned in the third stanza (one usually does not "sleep with quandariness") one sleeps from boredom and the lack of choice? but O'Hara wants to suggest connections between multiplicity, lack of connections guiding choice and forms of death); he encounters probably for the hundredth time a bank teller he has no communication with, yet who also disproves his expectations; and even the apparently most arbitrary item, the reference to Bastille day, has a curious appositeness in a poem so thoroughly about death, separation, and the fragility of established order. Moreover, the "and" rhetoric so pronounced in the poem further enhances one's sense of the tangential and problematic links between particulars: parataxis calls attention to the rush of time piling up details united only by sequential time alien to more discerning, specifically human patterns of relationship. The rush of life then embodies also a process of continual death leading to the climactic stoppages of life and breath in the last four lines. But the initial twenty lines also allows the poet to find a meaning in Billie's death, to see in her art and his memories of it the experience of connection which counters and helps mollify the pains of discontinuity. What he remembers about Billie is a moment of stasis that is at once death and very intense life —death because it so divorces him from the normal (and insignificant) activities of his daily life, and intense life for precisely the same reason since it has been that life which is really involvement in continual deaths. The moment he remembers is one of absolute communication when Billie controlled the entire audience and led them to a single ecstasy ("everyone and I stopped breathing"). And O'Hara's poem is itself an act like Billie

Holliday's; the full elegiac effect depends on our union with his memory. Like her singing the poem also can claim at least for a moment to transcend the contingent multiplicities of daily experience and, through the poem's deliberate slowing in these last lines, allow a brief space where we all stop that rushing breath always associated with process in O'Hara and realize how art and memory can console us in the face of recurrent death."

Altieri, Charles. "The Significance of Frank O'Hara." *The Iowa Review* 4.1 (1973): 90-104.

The Editor thanks Kate Conlow, Assistant Managing Editor, *The Iowa Review*, for her assistance, and especially thanks Dr. Charles Altieri for permission to republish excerpts from his article on Frank O'Hara.

Charles Altieri is the Rachel Stageberg Anderson Professor and Chair in the Department of English at the University of California, Berkeley. On his faculty webpage, he comments: "I have been primarily interested in the varieties of Twentieth Century American poetry, especially in relation to philosophy and to the visual arts."

MARGE PIERCY

Hopwood Awards: 1954; 1956; 1957

Email to Donald Beagle:

Answers to Questions for Book About Major Hopwood Winners

Did your Hopwood award impact your approach to subsequent work?

The main effect winning a major Hopwood had on me was that I could afford to go to France with the guy I was seeing, a French grad student in particle physics. Because of the money, I spent the summer with him and then married him. A major mistake but I learned a lot about myself from the whole experience. He viewed my writing as a nice hobby I would surely give up as I gave him the requisite number of babies.

His conservative attitude toward sex roles was not evident when he was a student. But as soon as we married, the traditional rules and expectations came out of hiding. What the whole experience taught me was 1. How American I am. 2. That my writing is the primary thing in my life, not secondary to any relationship. We were divorced two years later. 3. I can't play the standard wife role.

I appreciated the confidence the awards I won gave me, the vindication as a poet and fiction writer, four awards in all over my undergraduate years culminating in the major my senior year.

No, what I wrote as an undergraduate did not lead to my later work in poetry, but did in fiction. In several ways, the poems in my freshman Hopwood manuscript were closer to what I wrote later than the poems in my major manuscript. I did publish some of the earlier work later on, some in EARLY GRRRL. A few of the poems in my major collection were published in slightly different form in zines. But by the time my first collection BREAKING CAMP was accepted, I'd been writing lots of poetry for over a decade so I had many new poems to form the collection.

I began to publish individual poems by the time I graduated, slowly here and there over the years before my first collection eleven years later. it was much harder to get recognition for my fiction, since I was writing about women in a serious and sometimes political way, often workingclass women. No publisher was interested until the sixties created an opening for fiction like mine. I remember one agent saying to me in NYC, why are you writing about all this stuff? Why don't you write a nice love story? I could sell that.

I knew what I had to write, so I did.

Andrea Beauchamp once said that Hopwood winners seem to fall into two groups when they re-read their student manuscripts: pleasantly surprised, or unpleasantly disappointed.

I partly answered that question above. I've never read through my major poetry manuscript. I've looked at individual poems. I have a copy of it someplace in the house, although I'm not sure where. I have read through my earlier award winning fiction manuscript and have revised a couple of them for publication. But again, by the time I could publish my short stories [because there were women's liberation journals in existence for a period of about ten years], I was a far more mature writer and had lots of new stories to send out.

Which poets have influenced your own approach to writing poetry—ranging from "classics" to any contemporaries who may have influenced your mature work? Also, did any so-called "schools" of poetry impress you? Third (and last), are you aware of (or care to share) any non-literary influences that have been especially important to your writing: music, visual art, social change, environmentalism, etc.?

I think influences are a matter of adolescence and / or early adulthood. By the time you've matured as a writer, you go on pushing your art, trying to do more and more, taking on more difficult subjects, trying out voices, always continuing to develop your ear. You might get an 'idea' from another writer. I remember hearing June Jordan reciting "Getting down to get over" and thinking, I could write that honestly about my mother, her poverty, her struggles, her anger, her contradictions, her inability to love me after puberty until she was old. And I began to write strong poems about my mother and have never stopped since.

I don't think that's what I meant about influences when I was adolescent, especially Walt Whitman and Emily Dickinson. I didn't have any urge to write like June. It was like the revelation I had when I first heard Ginsburg read. Wow, I could write honestly about my sexuality, my Jewishness, my left politics. I don't have to pretend to be an Anglo Saxon male. I don't have to pretend to be repressed. Why write poems about seeing artwork when I could write about being in a protogang on the streets of Detroit, about my parents catching my older brother fucking his girlfriend on the livingroom couch and making them get married, about my uncle Zimmy the coalminer and Sunday poacher. I'd been taught every poem had to be 'universal' which meant it should sound like it was written by a white male – unless it was a love poem or a poem about missing a male lover. I began to write openly Jewish poems and indeed I've written liturgy that's used in Reform and Reconstructionist synagogues and Liberal congregations in the U.K. as well as UU congregations here. I could write about Pesach, my favorite holiday.

Everything in daily life influences me. After I moved to outer Cape Cod in 1971 when all my life up to that point had been in the center of cities, I began to write about the moon, the tides, the birds and animals and trees and weather. The seasons impact me heavily, especially since Ira Wood and I are serious gardeners who grow 90% of our vegetables. I don't know if I had ever looked closely at a bird or a squirrel or a raccoon or fox before I lived here. We live in the woods and a mile and a half from the ocean. Climate change is very real and evident here as are the effects of pollution. issues of water and land use, a dangerous rattletrap nuclear power plant run for profit and never safety by a corporation in New Orleans – all these impact us and thus my writing. Furthermore runaway real estate prices fueled by second homes barely lived in are preventing people from being able to live here – including many who were born here and grew up here. The horrible racist immigration policies of Trump are killing businesses here and preventing the influx of seasonal workers, many of whom stay on and become valuable parts of our communities, marrying, raising children: the kind of families Trump wants to break up and destroy.

Then there's the news I get every day off a number of sources on the internet. The anger I feel at injustice, racism, warmongering, economic deprivation, danger to women, ridiculously expensive medicine and health care – all that impacts me. All that enters my writing.

My feminism has strongly influenced my writing as it does my activism. I don't know how to weigh my various activisms against each other in importance: women's right to choose, equal pay, safety from rape and abuse, better maternal care, day care that's affordable; fighting against pollution of the air and water, the ocean, fighting against Pilgrim nuclear power plant, a clone of the Fukushima disaster plants but even worse maintained and run; fighting against all the disasters Trump is causing to citizens and noncitizens who aren't billionaires.

Have you found poetry readings to be useful or enjoyable? Have you been at all attracted to, or intrigued by, the option of sharing poetry (or musings about poetry) online via social media or similar digital venues?

I love giving readings. The travel is less pleasant and gets worse every year. Flying is like being loaded into a crowded garbage truck.

I believe poems are made of sounds and silence. I always hear my poems even if I'm not reading them out loud. But when I first perform a poem for an audience, I hear things that need fixing. Maybe a line comes apart like a broken string of pearls – usually because there are too many unaccented syllables. Maybe the metaphor is too forced. Maybe the poem needs more work on its oral qualities. Maybe it needs to be shortened or it needs more development in its trajectory. I hear what needs work when I perform the poem for the first time.

I contribute frequently to online zines. I see no difference between publishing poetry in hard copy journals and publishing poetry in online zines except that most times, more people read the online zines.

People pirate my poems all the time on sites and on Facebook. At first I tried to stop it but I've given up. I try to be happy that so many people want to share my work. What can I do?

Do you see modern academia in general as a good professional base for working poets? Do you feel the role of the poet in the academy has had any discernible impact—positive or negative—upon poetry in general?

I think the inability of writers in general to make a living on serious writing now has had a terrible impact on all of us. More and more sites expect writers to pay them to read the work instead of paying us to publish it. We're no longer poets or authors: just providers of content.

So the vast majority of writers, both poets and fiction writers, take university jobs.

The typical bio of a writer in my early adulthood would read: Joe Schmo worked oil rigs in Gulf of Mexico, crewed on a lobster boat in Maine, hunted wolves in Alaska and spent five years at a Tibetan monastery studying deep meditation before eloping with a Tahitian princess. Now Joe Schmo's bio would read: JS got his MFA at Iowa, had residencies at the Fine Arts Work Center in Provincetown and MacDowell. then joined the faculty of the University of Podunk Idaho, followed by a two year stint at Farthest Community College in Utah.

The problem: Joe used to meet and get to know people with many different jobs, people of various social classes, nationalities, races. Each of those environments gave him stories. His life with rich with experiences. it helps a writer to know how people behave in extreme situations. Maybe it even helps to have faced real danger. [I sound like Hemingway!] I'm biased. Maybe I'm just saying, *live like me*. And why should anyone? Except I've enjoyed my life and have few regrets.

Joe now goes from one college town to another, deals with English department faculty and writers and aspiring writers. He learns writing that is most valued is that on which a PhD thesis can be written. He learns that more accessible writing, writing that nonacademics find important to them, is scorned. He then writes for other poets and academics and collects prizes for poems no one else will ever read.

That's why I live in a village out to sea where my friends include a shellfish farmer, a shopkeeper, a bank manager, a lighthouse docent, DJs at the community radio station, a few poets, painters and fiction writers, local politicians, an osteopath, a mapmaker, a ship's captain, the owner and manager of a local cemetery, a carpenter, a builder, a chef, a housecleaner and a beekeeper. Their friendships and their stories enrich me and my writing.

[**Editor's Note**: Excerpt from an earlier interview with Marge Piercy]

"When asked whether women write differently from men, Piercy answered as one who has thought about the question: 'In a book by a woman, rape won't be fun and women won't be simple-minded. There are women who do the chic violence number; Jayne Anne Phillips writes like a man when she writes about miners. When she writes about people she knows, she writes like a woman.' Piercy believes that women writers in general, 'like Joanna Russ, are concerned with violence in a more real, ethical, troubled way.' When I asked whether women rely more on memory than men, she at first demurred. 'You can't claim that for women; Proust has a patent on memory and so does Joyce.' She went on to speak of memory as a storehouse of experience: 'You have to train yourself to remember; everything is in there if you can get at it. It's never all available to you. Your mind is a cantankerous old computer that doesn't remember how to access the old files. There are learned ways to access it; there's a discipline by which you can recapture it.'...."When Piercy received the Sheaffer-PEN/New England Award for Literary Excellence at the end of May 1989, she read from her poem 'The fecund complain they are not honored.' While the poem is about all writers with high productivity, it is also a self-description:'The driven work. They get up like Sylvia / Long before dawn. They write in buses. / They write in the laundromat while clothes / flash by, and somebody steals their socks. / They write on computers if one is there; / If not, they write in pencil or crayon.' The poem ends,'When the driven die / their real inner stone reads: you did / a little piece of it, a little piece.' Readers of Marge Piercy might disagree, believing she has already done more than a "little piece" of that work dictated by her conscience, her integrity, and her artistic genius."
----Quoted from: Pearlman, Mickey and Katherine U. Henderson. *Inter/View : Talks with America's Writing Women*. The University Press of Kentucky, 2015.

[This excerpt of 328 words is reproduced here under provision of Academic Fair Use.]

NANCY WILLARD

Hopwood Awards: 1955; 1956; 1957; 1958

Questions You Asked, Answers Nancy Willard Never Gave

By Eric Lindbloom

No doubt, Nancy's winning a Hopwood Award in each of her four undergraduate years had to come as confirmation of the path she was on. She'd been writing since childhood and published in the children's literature magazine, *Horn Book*. In high school, she'd won so many Scholastic Writing Awards, they devised a special award for her in the spring of 1953, when she was in the 11th grade at University High.

In our undergraduate days, in the mid-1950's, there was a vibrant student literary mix in Ann Arbor. The Hopwood Awards had a clear role in creating it. Anne Stevenson and Marge Piercy were students then. Both the literary magazine, *Generation*, edited by Piercy and myself in 1956-57, and the humor magazine, *Gargoyle*, staffed by Janet and Donald Malcolm, were engaging — with the edge going to *Gargoyle*. Nancy gained much from writing classes with the poet, Radcliffe Squires.

Having won a Major Hopwood Award in her senior undergraduate year, Nancy could not enter again in her graduate school days. She went to Stanford, earned a M.A. in medieval literature. While there she took a writing course with Yvor Winters, and managed to survive it.

Returning to Michigan to work on her Ph.D., she took her father's advice, and concentrated solely on writing the dissertation. But it was hardly a vacation from thinking about poetry. In her dissertation, later published as *Testimony of The Invisible Man*, she traced a common theme in the works of four poets, Neruda, Rilke, William Carlos Williams, and Francis Ponge. They all preached a poetics of putting aside the self, all the travails of the ego, and giving attention to the things of this world. Cleansing the doors of perception, suspending preconceptions, intense scrutiny. And then finding language, often metaphors, to share enlightened perceptions. It was Neruda's 'Elemental Odes' that chiefly formed a model that she wished to – and often did – follow.

In our graduate school days, the literary community in Ann Arbor was richer. Our friends, poets Jerry Badanes and Konstantinos Lardas, were both drawn there by the lure of the Hopwood Awards, as were, if I'm not mistaken, our friends the writers Padma Hejmadi and Victor Perera. Playwright and novelist Carl Ogelsby and poet Patricia Hooper rounded out our circle. There were some memorable long evenings in Ogelsby's basement study listening to him reading, in his southern drawl, from a novel in progress. Poets X. J. Kennedy and Keith and Rosmarie Waldrop were also at the University at this time. Donald Hall was teaching in the English Department and served on Nancy's dissertation committee.

I'd be amiss if I didn't mention a *Generation* Editor, George Abbot White. He did the unimaginable; he convinced the Board of the Office of Student Publications to fund the publication of four hard-back poetry books, including shortly after their college days, first books by Anne Stevenson, Konstantinos Lardas, and Nancy.

Nancy's early favorite poets were Marianne Moore and Richard Wilbur. In addition to the four poets studied in her dissertation, a few of the poets of her own generation she greatly admired were Denise Levertov, W. S. Merwin, Galway Kinnell, and Wislawa Szymborska. And then there's William Blake and Emily Dickinson! A Hudson Valley poet and wit, Mikhail Horowitz, introducing Nancy at a Woodstock Poetry Festival reading, said "Whenever I think of Nancy

Willard, I always imagine that somehow William Blake and Emily Dickinson got together in Heaven and produced a daughter."

Though firmly denying that she was a visual artist, Nancy was one. She made drawings, paintings, handmade books, soft sculpture, and later in life, the most ornately repurposed, old, drop-sided toasters. All this, she said, was just handwork while thinking about the current writing project. I don't know that Nancy had any position on the question of 'The Writer as College Teacher,' but I do know that she found the 47 years teaching at Vassar a balancing anchor outside of home and her writing desk. She loved the contact with perennially young and bright students. And she soon learned the trick of ducking committee work.

Nancy was slow to take up the computer, but once she did, she was quick to realize its advantages, no more white-out, no more retyping. Her laptop was not connected to the internet, but was simply a word-processor. We had another computer in the house that was connected, which she used to contact students, colleagues, editors. She was never tempted to sharing her poems via social media.

As I suspect with many poets, when it felt like time to assemble a new poetry manuscript, she gave a second look at all the poems she'd written since the last book, and selected those that survived a more critical reading. Ann Close, her long-time editor at Knopf, had a hand in this. Nancy loved giving poetry readings; fortunately, from early on, there were invitations. And readings were useful: an audible murmur would give some sense of the audience's response to a poem. One of my favorites, was a reading by Stanley Kunitz, Galway Kinnell, and Nancy on the occasion of a William Blake exhibition at The Metropolitan Museum of Art. Though I could as easily choose one of the last readings she gave, at Vassar, after the publication of *The Sea at Truro* in 2012. The auditorium was full, in near equal numbers, with students, faculty, and community members. Who knew it would be one of her last.

All of the above is suspect – except for statements of public record – absent Nancy Willard's take on things and her dulcet voice. *Viva* the Hopwood Awards.

[Eric Lindbloom thoughtfully sent this "briefest bio," adding that he uses "awful" in its archaic sense: "Eric Lindbloom and Nancy Willard lived and worked together in awful harmony for many years until her death in February 2017."]

Excerpt from the Introduction to Nancy Willard's collection *In His Country*

By Radcliffe Squires

"It will be evident to anyone reading *In His Country* that Nancy Willard is not *just* another poet. She is a poet of subtle idiosyncrasies, snappish individuality. And nowhere does one feel her individuality more strongly than in the very places where he is most aware that the great resonances of Rilke and the *Neue Gedicte* tutor Miss Willard's sensibilities. For the influence is admitted as an element, something to breathe or drink or move through; as necessary as that, but not more necessary than that. The breathing, the drinking, the moving are her own poetic transactions.

And what brilliant transactions! How beautifully she permits us to see into the life of things when she observes "dragonflies / thin as barometer's blood…"or when she observes:

> Saint Nicholas is the Patron Saint of
> children and scholars, by virtue
> of a subtle likeness
> acknowledged by neither.

Both these observations are inviolably true, yet they did not even exist before Nancy Willard made them exist.

I could pile up many such examples, but the reader can find his own. And, anyway, Miss Willard's poetry is not simply superb observations. It is much more than that. It is reality held together by forces strong enough to hold a sky together. But not terrifying forces. *In His Country* is—imagine it, please—demonically possessed by joy and goodness. It is haunted by angels."

[This excerpt of 228 words is reproduced here under provision of Academic Fair Use.]

Nancy Willard: A Guest Essay

By Theodore Haddin

Any reader who approaches the poetry, fiction and essays of Nancy Willard will discover a complex poet, who, like the magician of her stories, possesses the secrets of things, not so much for their tricks, as for their hidden meanings. When they come forth in the extraordinary accomplishment of her imagination in her poetry, we begin to think of William Butler Yeats and Wallace Stevens, perhaps Edgar Allan Poe. Yet she herself chooses to remain hidden, like the four poets of her book, *Testimony of the Invisible Man* (Missouri, 1970). This invisibility is there to promote the ascendancy of the things (or persons) she perceives. Her striking, one-poem biography of Emily Dickinson portrays the Dickinson who has not yet realized the important role consciousness will play in her poetry ("Transcript, 1848)." But Willard, by enjoining selflessness, is already a consciousness awaiting words.

In a spring morning of 1956, when I came out of my rooming house on Forest Avenue in Ann Arbor, I saw in the distance a girl with long hair on a bicycle with a large dog. Sunlight made her appear angel-like, and you don't forget someone who looks like an angel, if indeed there could be one in front of you. Nancy Willard was on her way to the woods and the road along the Huron River. On her return later our conversations would take us as far as the Hopwood Room in Angel Hall where she was reading manuscripts and writing her poetry. She was already a sophisticated poet. I was writing graduate papers on Wordsworth and George Eliot. Directed by Mary Cooley, the Hopwood Room had a good selection of books, and it was quieter than the library.

But where was her poetry coming from? Apparently her interests were so diverse, you couldn't easily answer this question. One evening she invited me to a Quaker meeting where we sat in a circle in the dark, waiting for someone to speak. Since Quakers believe that God is within us, speaking will bring out the Divine meanings associated with equality, simplicity, peace, love, and truth. Above all, participants accept selflessness. At that time in the University, you could be a "Zen" or a "Freud." Transcendental meditation was not yet the wave, but Quaker meetings were a form of communal meditation which could be very stimulating. In literature Cleanth Brooks had declared that poetry is the language of analogy, and Marianne Moore's "live toad in the imaginary garden" was to become Willard's lifelong mantra. At another meeting we heard Ralph Rabinovitch, a well-known psychiatrist who also consulted at a summer camp for adolescents near Ann Arbor. The focus could have been right on the Quaker emphasis on children and their mothers. The University Art Museum ran a fascinating exhibit of William Blake's engravings.

However much these experiences might have influenced Willard, she was not destined to be a Quaker poet or a Freudian, she was a *poet* wholly, in the true sense of the word. It is easier to see how she was influenced by her then mentor, Radcliffe Squires, who had arrived on campus only a few years earlier. I knew Radcliffe most of his writing life, had even taken his course in which we studied Blake. In his creative writing role, he was all creativity; in his presence you couldn't rely just on what you'd been reading. You had to speak from your own self, your own thoughts that could somehow become a poem. There was always a quiet urgency, as of someone intently listening.

Something of Radcliffe's influence may be seen in her poem, "Fairy Tale": "And if a white bear steps from the morning's throat/ may I be still enough to hear him/ may I be warm enough to invite him in." Radcliffe's "Animal Crossing" offers, "Then let me, animals, let me who motionless/ Lie athwart the road, let me be the path you cross. . . Let the little three-toed horse discover/ Footing between my ribs, and so cross over." It's the very touching devotion to the animal here that joins the writers. And there are other Willard poems like "Fontenen" (The Fountain) and "Kvinne og Enhjorning" (Woman and Unicorn) that resemble passages in Radcliffe's Garden poems. We are clearly in them when she writes, "Only the gods rise with the dew./ You must go through water to meet them,/ or at least be born in the image you grieve." She can write her "Swimming to China," and you know she's been reading Richard Wilbur's "Digging for China," but her poem is her own. Her "Guest" is perhaps there to tweak Robert Frost when she ends, "Come in."

More obvious are the poems of Pablo Neruda that enter her ken when she writes, for example, "In Praise of Unwashed Feet," and we read Neruda's "To the Foot from Its Child"; or her "My Life on the Road with Bread and Water" and Neruda's "Ode to Bread." But the poem that most shows how she could be inspired but move in a different direction is her "Walking Poem" and Neruda's sadly depressing lament about being a man, "Walking Around." Her poem is her happy self, a mother with her son on her back, where she ends with a stunning pun: ". . .we slip over the dark hill/ and I carry the sun away." (The son is still "sun.")

The voice in Nancy Willard's poetry differs little throughout her works, but the door between her poetry and stories and essays swings both ways. In one of her most original and humorous essays, "How Poetry Came into the World and Why God Doesn't Write It," she has God talking with Adam about a well over which Adam can say a word, and it will come up from the water so he can get approval from God himself who already knows about it. "That's nice," God would say. When Adam reads God a poem containing a metaphor, God approves, and the word comes into the world. When Adam is leaving the Garden, he laments that he will lose this well; but the angel tells him he hasn't lost it. "God doesn't want the well . . . The well is inside you . . . I hope you'll make some marvelous— 'Poetry'" Adam inserts.

This anecdotal story is what Willard likes to do—have someone else talk about what she values most so the reader gets another point of view for an explanation or truth-telling. This indirectly shows how much she values metaphor that is the major staple of all her poetry. Thus each of us can find amazing examples of it, like this one in "Flea Market": "eyeglasses . . . had come so far, like dinner plates/ gliding through portholes that leave behind/ the indestructible ship with its cargo of corpses." Or, in "The Potato Picker": "Sunflowers, kindly giants/ in their death-rattle turn stiff as streetlamps." And still, in one of her most celebrated, "The Patience of Bathtubs": "I have seen bathtubs like melancholy tureens/ into which the moon ladles her light broth." And last, but not least, a personification in "The Burning at Neilson's Farm" (in the Civil War): "Sprung/ birches fall into each other's arms,/ their torn jackets coiled, keeping the shape/ of broken logs rotting away inside."

Another poignant instance of her using, in this case material from her essay, "Close Encounters of a Story Kind," she describes an elderly man (a holocaust victim) who advises her concerning her lost manuscript about angels. Her experience with the man is so convincing, she gives up her idea of writing it and will start all over.

Meanwhile, she's very nearly convinced this soft-spoken and kindly visitor may be an angel himself, presenting the reader with the experience many people may have, of thinking there may be real angels, in this case, exploiting the Quaker notion that angels may be in the form of humans. She lists at least eleven different kinds of angels, from the angel of poetry to the angel of memory and the angel of time.

When we turn to the poetry, Willard expresses more than a fascination with angels, but we are ready for her. She starts with "My son and I lie down in white pastures/ of snow and flap like the last survivors/ of a species that couldn't adapt to the air," making angels in the snow but angels of themselves, and she realizes the similarity as if she had actually joined with the angel, for she says, ". . .I lift my body from the angel's," an instance in which she has more than figuratively experienced a thing in itself ("Angels in the Snow"). Later, when her son has purchased wings of an angel ("pressed from celluloid") to present on her birthday, she tries them on ". . . to buckle the wings to my body/ that never sprang from a sill/ or plotted the air through a thicket," she imagines how finely she could see herself as an angel ("The Winged Ones").

It is almost a finished fact for us to read how Willard describes unfeignedly the angel that first appeared in her grandmother's kitchen, then "at one o'clock in the front bedroom . . ./ to my grandmother who ". . . had lain down for a nap." Two hours later the gardener "saw a figure/ standing on top of the compost and found himself/ filled with such longing for another time and condition/ he burst into tears." The angel of this poem was seen no more, but everyone was uplifted; "for once in our world, everybody was happy" ("Memorial Day in Union City, Michigan").

A further instance of Willard's use of her prose occurs in her short story, "Sinner, Don't You Waste That Sunday." The Erica of the story, in offering an incredible account of her experience giving birth to a son, refers to "this secret she had carried so long," the thing *inside* that is as close to knowing the thing-in-itself she will ever know. At last, the two are one in the world, she can see, hear, feel, and taste part of her own life. We don't have to go far for the things Willard examines, like the fruit bat, the peacock, bees, the shark, insects, the moon snail, moss, the tortoise, fish, a dying goldfinch, even the onion, that she gives attention to in the poems. She is not the biologist or the zoologist who dissects a specimen (thing) to discover its anatomical structure.

She is the poet who reveals how a thing lives. *She* is most alive when she does this. But what do humans do, how do they *live*? What sort of thing are they? They get married in "Love in America"; they get pregnant in "For you, Who Didn't Know" where the Jewish doctor, (holding up his dobtone to test for fetus) profoundly answers to his Hasidim, "*What we say here is heard there.*" We don't have the birth in the poems, but the hospital, the preparation, the delivery room, the actual birth, in the story.

In the essay "Close Encounters of the Story Kind," her mother, losing her mind in a convalescent home suddenly recalls how her grandmother at a pump on a farm poured cold water on her wrists, how cold it felt, "how good it tasted." In the poem "Cold Water" Willard finds a stream in the woods and becomes totally absorbed in it, "I plunged my face in and drank. . . . My tongue scrolled up water. . . .I rolled the stream in my mouth . . . .I savored my own birth./ I cupped my hands and sipped." Without a priest, she experiences a natural baptism "as if I could. . . save contentment for when I'd need it." And she *knows* water. As if she couldn't get close enough to cold water to *be* the thing, aided by metaphor she *is* the thing she describes in the brief poem "Marriage Amulet":

> You are polishing me like old wood.
> At night we curl together like two rings
> on a dark hand. After many nights,

> the rough edges wear down.
> If this is aging, it is as warm as fleece.
> I will gleam like ancient wood.
> I will wax smooth, my crags and cowlicks
> well-rubbed to show my grain.
> Some sage will keep us in his hand for peace.

Nancy Willard's wit and humor can pull a reader in when she puts the question of the thing-in-itself in the voice of another person, (as mentioned above), in this instance an old man, the Yiddish vegetable man in "Roots."

Behind the mask of the vernacular, perhaps her only vernacular poem, he celebrates the potato, a master of salesmanship:

> Potatoes you need, maybe?
> My wife says I eat too many
> potatoes. In Poland, in war
> we ate potatoes, soup
> baked, boiled
> All my family was ploughed under
> except me. So what can I say
> to someone that he don't like
> potatoes? Positively last chance,
> because tomorrow it might snow.
>
> In winter I don't come. . . .
>   . . .
> I'm eighty-two already
> and what is Paradise
> without such potatoes?

Even this humorous expression of the thing, however, doesn't keep her from having reservations about how she treats some things, as when she regrets having carved a pumpkin "because I gave you a false face/ and a light of my own making" ("Saint Pumpkin"). Or the utter quizzicalness she experiences when she's attempted to grasp a moon snail and is somehow perplexed at having touched it ("A Human Error"). Her profound reaction suggests not just that she should leave things alone, but that in both instances she has disrupted the life that was in the thing. To put it in her own words, she may have severed the "skin of grace." (See the poem.) But the overwhelming sense of reverence she expresses for nature and everything else moves through the poems, expresses her love that is immediate and goes beyond. At least five poems can tie her writing to St. Francis of Assisi, especially to his "Canticle of the Sun." Hers are: "Poem Made of Water," "Wreath to the Fish," "Carpenter of the Sun," "A Psalm for Running Water," and "The Animals Welcome Persephone."

Though blind, St. Francis dictated his "Canticle" (also known as "Praise of the Creatures") in which he celebrates Brother Sun, Sister Moon, stars, Brother Wind, air, Sister Water, Brother Fire, Sister Mother Earth, fruits, flowers, herbs, divine love, peace, and Sister Bodily Death. An important observation here is that his love for nature and all creatures "had grown into unity in his own heart" (Father Eric Doyle, *Wikipedia*). This indeed, is the poet we know, Nancy Willard. The title of her novel, *Sister Water* hints at the connection with St. Francis that runs through all her works. The reference to the heart echoes her comment, "What does it mean to enter the nature of a thing? When a haiku master enters the heart of a thing, the distinction between subject and object disappears" (*Testimony*, 100). The selflessness does not exclude the heart, but makes her love eventuate in a poem like "Poem Made of Water" that puts her own life once more into her praise for water:

> Praise to my text, Water, which taught me writing,
> and praise to the five keepers of the text,
> Water in Ocean, water in River, water in Lake,

> water in cupped hands, water in Tears. Praise
> for River, who says: travel to the source,
> poling your craft of words, mindful of currents,
> avoiding confusion, delighting in danger
> when its spines sparkle, yet keeping
> your craft upright, your sentence alive.
> You have been sentenced to life. (ll. 1-10)

This is not only in praise of water, but a mandate for the poet's writing life. In "A Visit to William Blake's Inn" life indeed may be required to walk the Milky Way with William Blake ("I fear we may finish it old," says Blake), but it will be the journey of a lifetime with the animals, and worth all the praise she might make and spiritual enquiry she might encounter. In the "Epilogue" to this poem it's indeed as if in returning, she's coming to the end of her life. So she nostalgically says, "My adventures now are ended," and:

> You whose journeys now begin,
> if you reach a lovely inn,
> if a rabbit makes your bed,
> if two dragons bake your bread,
> rest a little for my sake,
> and give my love to William Blake.

Theodore Haddin, Writer, Editor
Associate Professor Emeritus, UAB, Birmingham, Alabama

KEITH WALDROP

Hopwood Award: 1958

A Few Fragments for an Imperfect Memoir of Keith Waldrop

By X. J. Kennedy

In all my years, I have met no one more remarkable than Keith Waldrop, no one of such unique and varied accomplishments. Keith has excelled as a poet, a writer of prose, a translator, an editor, a publisher, a teacher, a director and producer of plays, and a successful hoax-stager. On first getting to know him, I was struck by his seeming to have read everything, both foreign and domestic. For him literature has long been a large and vital art of life. He has absorbed books for pleasure, never from duty, and wears his learning lightly. As a teacher, that was how he taught. When he was nearing his retirement from Brown, I was surprised to learn that, when most aging professors slow down and feel like short-timers, Keith had begun teaching a new course in Restoration drama. "They didn't know it," he said of his students, "and somebody had to give it to them."

We first met as graduate students in Ann Arbor, when Keith needed somebody to help him move his burgeoning collection of books to new quarters. I don't know why he asked me, for we were only slightly acquainted, but I agreed, for Keith has always had a talent for persuasion. After he and the books made the move we stood and talked for a couple of hours. We had both been students in France, where I had picked up a copy of Samuel Beckett's novel *Watt*, and this fact made me a person of interest. A further bond was that we both loved Alfred Jarry's offensive play "Ubu Roi," and felt it needed staging.

This conversation led to a few collaborations, the first of which was a hoax. Beat poetry was new at the time, and no one in town quite knew what it was, so the moment seemed right to announce a reading by three beatniks from San Francisco. To play one of the parts, Keith disguised himself by shaving off his beard; another grad student stained his face and hands to look African-American; and a Waldrop woman friend from Detroit was enlisted, for no one in Ann Arbor would know her. I acted as master of ceremonies, and Keith set up some distinguished professors to ask questions from the floor. He also borrowed a service revolver from the Ann Arbor police, who apparently didn't expect him to stick up a gas station. When the appointed night came, the Rackham lecture hall was jammed with the curious. A seductive girl undergraduate was engaged to sit in a front row. She wore short shorts and went barefoot, and caused male tongues to hang out. The pseudo beat poets did their things, and the evening concluded with their reading "The Quivering Aardvark and the Jelly of Love," a bad Victorian American play that we had jazzed up with what we imagined was beat vocabulary. At its end, Keith whipped out the service revolver, cried, "And here's one for that gah damned aardvark," and fired two blanks over the heads of the audience. In that low-ceilinged room, the sound was devastating. Then someone shut off the lights, and the whole cast made their escape, leaving the audience sitting for several minutes in the dark. Afterward one spectator was heard to say, "That was terrific, man. All that poetry and then—nothingness." For days afterward, people argued whether or not the event had been for real.

The success of this hoax encouraged Keith to produce and direct plays. Next, he staged Jarry's "Ubu Roi," titled "Go-potty Rex." He translated half of it and I, the other half, so we wouldn't have to pay a permission fee. The play is a loose travesty of "Macbeth," with a conspiracy to seize the throne of Poland. I played the cruel and stupid Papa Go-potty and Keith his mate, Mama. The audience on one side of the arena threw Polish sausage at the actors and the audience on the other side threw it back. That night we had to scrape crushed sausage off the groundcloth of the stage; still, the enlightened head of the drama department let us give the show for a second night as had been planned. Once again Keith introduced a police revolver, and there was a small live orchestra. with Rosmarie Waldrop on flute.

Keith followed that with more plays, notably Beckett's "Endgame," and then "The Talking Ass" by visiting professor John Heath-Stubbs, based on the Biblical story of Balaam. Fellow grad student Bill Kenny and I played the ass, with a blanket tossed over us. I got to do the talking; my part was billed as First half-ass. Then, Keith staged Christian Dietrich Grabbe's "Comedy, Satire, Irony, and Deeper Meaning," in which I played a pompous pedagogue; and Paul Goodman's "Jonah," in which Dorothy Kennedy played a drunken sailor.

Keith and Rosmarie had met when the U.S. Army stationed him in her home town of Kitzingen, Germany; both became students in France, at the University of Aix-en-Provence. When Rosmarie came to Ann Arbor, she was a rule-observing churchgoer, and the priest wouldn't marry them until Keith had undergone Catholic instruction. Keith had rented a small house, and there the two of them lived, presumably as chastely as brother and sister, while the priest gave Keith some lessons. At last the morning dawned when I was awakened by a rattle of pebbles on the window of my upstairs bedroom. Keith stood below. The priest was ready to marry them but they needed a witness. I flung on my clothes and hightailed it to the church, where the wedding was performed during the break between two morning masses.

Its validity was immediately questioned. Lurking in the church had been another grad student, a dropout from a Jesuit seminary, who thought himself more Catholic than the Pope. He accosted the priest and cast doubt on my qualifications to have served as a witness, because he knew me for a fallen-away Catholic. To which the sensible priest replied, "Mind your own business."

When Dorothy and I were married, the Waldrops threw us a reception. Keith and Jim Camp created a huge wedding cake in the shape of a battleship, complete with sparklers. Camp accompanied it with a bowl of a powerful punch that had guests staggering. The Waldrops' little house on the side-street of Turner Park Court soon became a salon where literati hung out and poets met to share their work and criticize it. Books began to overflow the walls, and the place was patrolled by a large whale-shaped tomcat named Moby Dick, a wedding present from Keith's mother. At the poets' meetings, Dallas Wiebe, James Camp, and I were regulars, and a couple of times there were established poets —-Don Hall, brought to Michigan as a young associate professor, and De Snodgrass from nearby Wayne State. Unlike Dorothy and me, Keith and Rosmarie actually achieved their PhDs, with Keith writing a dissertation whose topic, obscenity in literature, was accepted by the conservative English department only because it was championed by star scholar and critic Austin Warren. I trust that department chairman Warner G. Rice later heard that Keith had become director of graduate studies in English at Brown. The news must have shocked him to the core.

Both Keith and Rosmarie went on to become celebrated nontraditional poets. From Keith's long bibliography, a good introduction would be his *Selected Poems* (Omnidawn, 2016), together with the collage poems *Transcendental Studies* (University of California Press), which copped the 2009 National Book Award for poetry. Although those collections are what might be called experimental poetry, I am also fond of Keith's many songs, notably one that begins "Pippin my garbageman is dead."

Not only have the Waldrops produced a large and impressive body of ground-breaking poetry of their own, they have fostered it (and experimental prose) in scores of titles churned out for more than a half-century by their small press Burning Deck. It would be hard to overestimate the influence of that publishing operation.

As a translator, Keith is distinguished, having Englished poets such as Claude Royet-Journoud, Anne-Marie Albiach, and Edmond Jabès; not to mention Charles Baudelaire —Keith rendered the entire *Flowers of Evil* into remarkably poetic prose (Wesleyan University Press, 2005). The French government has appreciated the Waldrops' efforts by giving them both medals and the rank of Chevalier des arts et des lettres.

Any list of Keith's accomplishments has to include his great *Light While There Is Light: An American History*, a slightly fictionized autobiography. Much of it deals with his family—dysfunctional, to say the least—and portrays his incompatible parents, who eventually separated. His mother was a Fundamentalist who loved revival meetings and believed in divine healing, but Keith's father named him for two celebrated skeptics—Bernard for Shaw and Keith for Sir Arthur Keith. Keith's mother was convinced that her husband had chosen the names of "two old atheists" just to irritate her.

She had had three children by her first husband: Elaine, a sweet and sensible woman; Charles, who seems never quite to have got his life under control; and Julian, something of a rascal. He once peddled warm watermelons through the streets of Atlanta, claiming they were ice cold; and later ran a business in Urbana, Illinois, called Used Car Heaven. He deserted from the Air Force only to be tracked down by the FBI and sentenced to Leavenworth.

Keith's seldom saw his father, Arthur Waldrop, after his parents' separation, but the old man's had a profound influence on him. A lover of Shakespeare's plays who knew several of them practically by heart, he took young Keith to see "Hamlet"—for the boy "a view into another realm, a realm infinitely appealing and, most surprisingly, available..."

I should add one further accomplishment: Keith's discovery of John Barton Wolgamot. Once while he skimmed the shelves of a used book store, his eye stopped on an odd-shaped elongated volume by Wolgamot, entitled *In Sara, Mencken, Christ, and Beethoven There Were Men and Women*. This curious tome devotes each page to a scrupulously accurate list of the names of celebrities, ending either "very titanicly" or "very majestically." Keith founded a John Barton Wolgamot Society, whose members are automatically inducted for life if they merely behold a page of the holy book.

Close Listening with Keith Waldrop 2009

[**Editor's Note**: The following has been excerpted from "Close Listening with Keith Waldrop," (an interview with the poet conducted soon after his book, *Transcendental Studies*, won the 2009 National Book Awards for Poetry) recorded November 5, 2009, as one of a series of "Close Listening" conversations at the Kelly Writers House for PennSound and Art International Radio. Waldrop was interviewed by Charles Bernstein. This excerpt of 276 words is reproduced here with permission of Rosmarie & Keith Waldrop, and interviewer Charles Bernstein.]

Waldrop: "*Transcendental Studies* is probably my only full book that is basically collage poems. I started doing them because I had to become the director of a program [at Brown University].....And Brown, yes, in the writing program. I found that — it wasn't that the job was difficult — but it was one of those endless things where you keep thinking, you try to think of anything, you think, tomorrow I must do this or yesterday I should've done this, and I found I wasn't writing any poetry, and so I decided I must. There are various ways of writing poetry. Well, in any way you write poetry, there are certain amounts of drudgery to it, of doing some things that are not part of really, you really don't have to think about. And for instance, if you're translating, just to get the meaning of the words, what does this text mean, and then you have to start really translating. So I decided I would do a kind of collage, and simply put some books out and get phrases from them and see what happened. And this was simply my way of finding poems, it wasn't that I was trying to do a particular kind of collage. I wasn't trying to prove anything about collage. Once the collage elements managed to make a stanza, let alone a poem, I would change things if I felt — well that word isn't good, I'd rather have this other word. And someone who is passionate about, you know, this is supposed to be collage, would say, "That's not fair." But I didn't really think anything about collage; I wanted to find poems."

X. J. KENNEDY

Hopwood Award: 1959

The Hopwood Experience

To be sure, winning a Hopwood poetry prize gave me a tremendous boost in morale. It also gave me a bigger piece of cash than I had ever had in my hand before, but what mattered more, it placed my work before influential judges—Louise Bogan, astute poetry reviewer for *The New Yorker*, and editor Henry Rago. Bogan later reviewed my first book favorably; and when I submitted to Rago "Nude Descending a Staircase," a poem from the manuscript, he printed it in *Poetry* magazine.

I wasn't a rank beginner. Before coming to Michigan I had spent four years in the Navy as an enlisted man with little work to do and plenty of time to write. A bale of poems accumulated, without any pressure to publish, although just before becoming a civilian again I sent four poems to Howard Moss of *The New Yorker*, and damned if he didn't keep two of them. I didn't include those items in the Hopwood manuscript. That might have seemed showing off. I did subtitle the Hopwood entry "Poems 1952 – 1958" to show that I wasn't a spring chicken. Indeed, I was an old geezer of nearly 30.

John Ciardi once half-seriously proposed breaking into the Hopwood Room some night and destroying our winning manuscripts. I didn't share that urge. There were weak pieces in my winner, all right, but nothing I felt ashamed of, and the Hopwood manuscript became the basis of my first book. For the existence of that first book, I have the Hopwoods to thank. That spring, Naomi Burton, a literary agent, came to Ann Arbor to check out the winners, and she picked up my manuscript and tried to market it around New York. There were no takers, but by luck Naomi became a senior editor for Doubleday, and soon published my first collection.

That collection must have displayed many influences, that of Yeats most of all. But although you can learn much from studying Yeats's masterful uses of rhyme and meter, he is otherwise inimitable. I also love Blake's "Songs of Innocence and Experience," Emily Dickinson's and Gerard Manley Hopkins's work, W. D. Snodgrass's *Heart's Needle,* and everything by the late lamented Richard Wilbur. I don't believe I owe anything to any school, such as confessional poetry; but certainly owe much to being an ex-Catholic, inheriting a vast trove of symbolism and lore.

In assembling a collection, I've never especially cherished the sequence that poems are placed in. When I read a new book of verse, all that matters is whether there are any true poems in it. I have a rather down-to-earth view of the poet's art: making a poem is like a carpenter's making a cabinet. In the Hopwood manuscript there's a quatrain called "Ars Poetica":

> The goose that laid the golden egg
> Died looking up her crotch
> To find out how her sphincter worked.
> Would you lay well? Don't watch.

I do believe that the process of writing verse shouldn't be intellectualized, but left intuitive. You never know where it will lead, nor what you'll get.

For twenty-one years I taught college for a living, and was always grateful to the academe for enabling my family and me to eat. Eventually I quit teaching and wrote textbooks for a living, and that let me write other things as well, such as books of verse and fiction for children, and the widely ignored novel *A Hoarse Half-human Cheer*.

A Salute (Not a Threnody) for Joe Kennedy

By Cody Walker

X. J. Kennedy! The name alone, with that self-affixed *X*, gives a jolt of pleasure. Joe Kennedy's poems have provided untold pleasures for more than sixty years now. His "Epitaph for a Postal Clerk" (beginning "Here lies wrapped up tight in sod / Henry Harkins c/o God") first appeared in *The New Yorker* in 1956. His most recent collection, *That Swing* (containing, among other things, wondrous versions of Mallarmé and Laforgue), appeared in 2017. He's won a bushel of prizes, including the 2015 Jackson Poetry Prize. (From the judges' citation: "His subtly dissonant rhymes and side-stepping meters carry us through the realms of puzzlement and sorrow to an intimated grace. The size of his poems is small but their scope is vast.") He has also, as you read a page back, won a Hopwood Award. Or two.

Let's start with the Hopwoods. As Joe mentions in his preceding piece, his Hopwood Award–winning poetry manuscript formed the basis for his first published collection, *Nude Descending a Staircase* (a book that would go on to win the 1961 Lamont Poetry Prize from the Academy of American Poets). What he doesn't mention is that he won a second Hopwood, as well: the Major Award in the Essay. (One of the judges was Irving Howe.) The collection consists of two essays and a commonplace book, and it makes for tremendously entertaining reading. Since it's not readily available (unless you happen to find yourself in the Special Collections reading room in the University of Michigan's Hatcher Graduate Library), I'd like to share some favorite moments from it:

When I was first beginning to discover poetry, I had an idea that every poem should make the same kind of literal sense that a timetable does, or an almanac. The first time I read Wallace Stevens' "Emperor of Ice Cream," I felt a bit immoral for enjoying it.

What I didn't realize then is that poetry is a willing suspension of logic for the sake of beauty. This suspension of logic is limited to the duration of the poem, and mustn't be carried over into the practical supervision of one's life. Try to catch trains by Blake's "Tyger" and you'll end up either a militant mystic or a suicide.

***

A poem may be written in half an hour, and the preparing of it require half a life.

***

What is poetry? When I try to answer this question, I'm reduced to the plight of the man who was asked, What are colors? I won't undertake a definition—but I can show you some.

***

The only honest way I can think of to conduct a poem-writing course is the way Radcliffe Squires runs his at Michigan, I'm told: he makes all the belated Victorians write free verse and all the would-be wooly Whitmans write sonnets and madrigals. That's what such a course can be: a gymnasium of calisthenics to limber the stiff and toughen the flabby.

***

So much poetry these days is nothing but talk, talk, talk. I want to shout, Shut up and give us a song, you blatherers!

***

Amazing, right? And as far as I know, very few people have seen these sentences in years. I've been looking for a way to share them; I'm glad to be given the space to do so here.

But back to the poetry. The one thing everyone knows about Joe's poems is that they're funny. His first book offers sly turns and laugh-out-loud surprises. (From "Faces from a Bestiary": "Hyena is a beast to hate. / No man hath seen him copulate." From "King Tut": "And now King Tut / Tight as a nut / Keeps his big fat Mummy shut. // King Tut, / Tut, tut.") But it also offers poems that give pause and bring a chill. (See "Little Elegy," which starts, "Here lies resting, out of breath, / Out of turns, Elizabeth.") In this way, he's a bit like Frost, whom Joe met at Bread Loaf shortly before the publication of *Nude Descending a Staircase*. (I'm thinking of the Frost who wrote the rollicking "Provide, Provide," but also the Frost who wrote, say, "Acquainted with the Night.") This tonal toggling—the deadly funny mixed with the deadly serious—has continued throughout Joe's career. It's one of the things I like best about him.

His tonal range allows him to take on the largest subjects—Love, Death (Dickinson: "More than Love and Death? Then tell me its name!")—and keep readers guessing as to how the subjects will be treated. Some of his poems are entirely serious (though never, in a distinction he would hope to maintain, solemn): "Daughter in the House," "In a Secret Field," "Last Child," "Evening Tide," "September Twelfth, 2001." Others are wild larks. (See—and listen to!—these lines from "In a Prominent Bar in Secaucus One Day":

"Oh, I'd never sit down by a tumbledown drunk / If it wasn't, my dears, for the high price of junk.") And then there are poems like "A Little Night Music" (from the original Hopwood manuscript, though not published in a collection until more than a decade later). It ends: "In love we tune for death, / So if you're not averse, / My dear, undress. In bed / We'll dress-rehearse the hearse." Love and death. And funny! (In a ho ho, oh no, kind of way.)

W. C. Fields once said, "I never saw anything funny that wasn't terrible. If it causes pain, it's funny; if it doesn't, it isn't." Fields would have enjoyed, as do I, Joe's *Brats* poems (which are marketed as children's poetry, but which I teach all the time to my college students). Witness Philbert Spicer, who "peered into a cold-cut slicer." You can guess what follows: The slicer shaves "Fifty chips off Phil's old block, / Stopping just above the eyebrows. / Phil's not one of them there highbrows." Or enjoy Junior, who finds his father, a suicide, hanging "like some old coat." The poem concludes: "Junior runs to Mom to beg: / 'Let's take Poppa down a peg!'" Terrible, I say! And unlike 99% of the poetry I read, deeply funny and impossible to forget.

Of course, the terribleness of these scenarios is tempered by how preposterous they are. (Aristotle, in his *Poetics*, defines the comic mask as essentially ludicrous: something ugly and distorted that doesn't imply real pain.) Other poems of Joe's begin with a comic conceit that then gives way to moments more direct, more recognizably human. Take "To Dorothy on Her Exclusion from the *Guinness Book of World Records*," which kicks off with a list of outrageous feats (e.g., "having whacked from Meires to Madrid / The longest-running hoop") and ends like this: "you merely settle chin / Into a casual fixture of your hand / And a uniqueness is, that hasn't been." (That's a love sonnet that belongs in the canon of such sonnets.) And what about "Invitation to the Dance," a tale of a retirement facility gone berserk (resurrected?) on Easter morning, in which our heroine, the feeble Mabel O'Lannihan, cries, "It's no sort of Sunday to stay in a tomb. / This world is the worse for a shortage of dancing. / Stand back, you old pill, give me plenty of room!" It's a joke—but it's also, for Joe, a kind of mission statement.

"Invitation to the Dance" is a longish poem: seventy-two lines. Most of Joe's poems are much shorter than that, and in fact he has a whole collection of poems, *Fits of Concision*, that are six lines or fewer. In the preface to that collection, he writes: "Whenever I open a new book of poetry and spy an extremely short poem, I can't help myself—I read it immediately. There's something about it that calls for attention." I feel the same way, and perhaps you do, too. Does Oedipus really need more than three descriptors? Joe calls him a "Kingdom-killin / Mammyjammin / Poppa-bopper!" Could anthologized poems stand a bit of compression? Here's the first of Joe's "Famous Poems Abbreviated": "Of man's first disobedience and its fruit / Scripture has told. No need to follow suit." And here's the second: "Once upon a midnight dreary, / Blue and lonesome, missed my dearie. / Would I find her? Any hope? / Quoth the raven six times, 'Nope.'"

This is playfulness of the highest order. (Again, I think of Frost: "Play's the thing. All virtue in 'as if.'") Serious play involves establishing boundaries, producing patterns, and then extending or subverting those patterns. Joe is as well versed in this kind of play as any living poet: his metrical effects are deft; his rhymes are ever inventive. From "Close Call": "How suddenly she roused my ardor, / That woman with wide-open car door." He rhymes "weenie" with "Bellini" (and elsewhere: "monokini"). I can still remember the joy I felt opening *Poetry* magazine a little over a decade ago and finding these lines from Joe's "More Foolish Things Remind Me of You": "Loud slurping noises from the next apartment, / A critic's lecture on what Hitler's art meant." My test for a good poem is a simple one: Do I wish I had written it? In this case (and in so many others, when reading Joe's work): Yes, yes, a thousand times yes.

I've only met Joe once—fifteen years ago, in Seattle, when he and his wife Dorothy came in for the 2003 Roethke Memorial Poetry Reading at the University of Washington. We rode a ferry around Puget Sound all afternoon, and that evening Joe read and sang in front of an adoring crowd. I told him I had long used his invaluable textbook, *An Introduction to Poetry*, in my writing workshops. "Thanks for helping to put my kids through college!" he laughed. (He has a handful of children, and a handful-plus of grandchildren.) Years later, in 2016, I was putting together a class in Ann Arbor called "Michigan Poets, Then and Now." Digging through Special Collections, I found not only Joe's Hopwood manuscripts but also, to my delight, a mention of Joe in a 1962 letter from Roethke to Allan Seager (Roethke's friend and biographer). Roethke had written: "You might tell this guy X. J. Kennedy I used his book as a text in a verse-writing class. The kids liked him." So, *Nude Descending a Staircase* was taught in Seattle more than four decades before Joe arrived for that reading I witnessed. I sent Joe a copy of the letter and he replied, "Yes, it was news to me—news 55 years delayed!"

"One A.M. with Voices," the last poem in that first collection, imagines the poet up late, laboring over rhymes. His lover tries coaxing him to bed: "You shall have / The warmed side of the bed / That sleep may with a breath blow out / This guttering in your head." From our present vantage point, it's clear the invitation was never wholly successful. Joe's work—so much more than a guttering—has been, over the years, a bright candle. Never a "today-type guy" (to borrow a jab from one of his poems), he's a guy for the ages. He's lit the way for many of us.

***

Cody Walker teaches English and directs the Creative Writing Sub-concentration at the University of Michigan. He's the author of two full-length poetry collections, *Shuffle and Breakdown* and *The Self-Styled*

No-Child, as well as a chapbook, *The Trumpiad* (which doubles as an ACLU fundraiser). His work appears in *The New York Times Magazine*, *Slate*, and *The Best American Poetry* (2015 and 2007). Along with Laura Kasischke, he co-directs the Bear River Writers' Conference.

X. J. Kennedy comments about rhyme and meter in his poetry:

"Well it seems to me that when you write in meter and rhyme you erect obstacles between yourself and so-called 'self-expression.' I'm especially thinking of all the undergraduate poets I've worked with, or talked to, because when they first try writing in rhyme, they're appalled because they're unable to say what they wanted to say. So I try to explain to them that being unable to say exactly what our tight, little intellects want to say, is a great advantage—and that by coping with the arbitrary restrictions of form we can be led forward on a very curious and exciting voyage of discovery. Very often, the best poems are those that shape themselves unexpectedly. When you write in rhyme it's as if you're walking across a series of stepping stones into the darkness, and you can't really see what's on the far end of the stepping stones. So you're led onward, often to say things that surprise and astonish you. As Rolfe Humphries once put it, rhyme leads you to say much better things than you could have thought of all by yourself. And that's also, I believe, one of the ways in which form prevents us from waxing too personal. Nowadays, many poets write in free verse, and many of them have nothing to prevent them from gassing on cozily about their own little personal concerns. But rhyme and meter stand in the way of that kind of self-absorption, or at least, they make it more difficult. As W. D. Snodgrass has pointed out, the process of shaping a poem in a rhymed stanza can often force you to find out what you really want to say through the process of laboriously overcoming obstacles."

Fourteen on Form: Conversations with Poets. William Baer
Univ. Press of Mississippi, 2009. 276 pages
[This excerpt of 286 words is reproduced here under provision of Academic Fair Use.]

PATRICIA HOOPER

Hopwood Awards: 1960; 1961; 1962; 1963

Letter to Donald Beagle

Did your Hopwood award impact your approach to subsequent work?

It's been my experience that recognition inspires, and lack of it can stifle the spirit. If recognition comes early in life, so much the better, because it encourages a writer to persevere. Before I came to Ann Arbor, I had published poems in *The American Scholar* and *New Directions Anthology* while still in high school, but like most young writers, I was full of doubt. Winning Hopwood Awards gave me a vote of confidence, something I was going to need later when life pulled me in different directions, and making time to write became a challenge.

More important, though, was that the Hopwood Program included the Hopwood Room, which gave me a sense of community. Many writers gathered there once a week for the Hopwood teas, over which Mary Cooley, once a student poet herself, presided. It is hard for me to imagine that room without her hospitality and delightful presence. There I met Nancy Willard, Konstantinos Lardas and Anne Stevenson, all of whom were graduate students when I was an undergraduate. This is the first time I found myself among a group of poets, and it would be the last for about ten years.

Andrea Beauchamp once said that Hopwood winners seem to fall into two groups when they re-read their student manuscripts: pleasantly surprised, or unpleasantly disappointed.

I didn't save my Hopwood manuscripts but I'm sure I'd be disappointed if I saw them again. All of the Hopwood Awards I received came to me as an undergraduate, and these were the poems of adolescence. Whatever technical abilities I had far exceeded my knowledge and experience. It took another twenty years before my first book, *Other Lives*, was published, and only one of those early poems was included. In my sophomore year, John Frederick Nims, who was the editor of *Poetry*, served as a judge. He asked to publish one of the manuscript poems in *Poetry*, and when it came out a year later I saw only how flawed it was and began revising it immediately, right on the pages. Surgery couldn't save it. Obviously, this was not the poem that found its way into my first book.

Which poets have influenced your own approach to writing poetry—ranging from "classics" to any contemporaries who may have influenced your mature work? Also, did any so-called "schools" of poetry impress you?

I've always been an eclectic reader and enjoy individual poems from many different "schools". Most poets don't always fit entirely into the groups they profess to be part of or that we assign to them. When I was at Michigan, I was immersed in the so-called "confessional poets" who were popular at the time. But by my senior year I was aware of other possible kinds of writing emerging in the work of James Wright and Robert Bly. After graduation I spent several years studying Rilke and Akhmatova, learning how their poems were made. My concept of what poetry can do is always evolving.

Having written and published many individual poems, could you describe how your creative process extends to assembling a full collection for publication?

The process of assembling a poetry manuscript is similar, for me, to writing a poem. I would like the poems to add up to something I didn't quite anticipate beforehand. Like writing a poem, that process involves both reason and intuition. Although I'm choosing from a group of poems written during a specific time, I also want the poems to be loosely held together in terms of themes. Sometimes poems of a certain period don't quite fit, and I set them aside for another book. Often those poems are precursors of a different direction I want to explore, and I don't want to publish them until that impulse exhausts itself. Others may have appeared in magazines but are either not good enough or don't fit into any principle of organization, and these I leave out.

Have you found poetry readings to be useful or enjoyable? Have you been at all attracted to, or intrigued by, the option of sharing poetry (or musings about poetry) online via social media or similar digital venues?

I enjoy poetry readings but I don't write with them in mind. Poetry requires a certain kind of attention from both reader and writer, something rare in the age of technology, even more rare in a public place. I would like my poems to be read in solitude, one consciousness communicating with another.

When emotion is embodied in image, it can be shared, and that experience is why I read poetry in the first place. Having said this, at some time in the process of writing a poem I always read it aloud, either to myself or to my writing group. It helps me see whether or not there are any false sentiments or awkward phrases I might have overlooked.

Do you see modern academia in general as a good professional base for working poets? Do you feel the role of the poet in the academy has had any discernible impact—positive or negative—upon poetry in general?

I know only second-hand how teaching affects poets who work in academia. But I know that having poets in the academy is a good thing for students.

Poetry involves a way of thinking that differs from the kind we use every day. It goes beyond reason alone, and when it goes well it arrives at a kind of knowledge or realization we cannot come to by any other means.

A poet in the classroom can make students aware of how this mode of thought is operating in a poem, something other academics often miss. I studied with Donald Hall at Michigan, and most of what I know about poetry I learned from him, both from his classes and from his books.

[Editor's Note: "Patricia Hooper's poems of shimmering intelligence"]

By Dannye Romine Powell
Charlotte Observer
December 2, 2015

One of the most enriching events for the state of North Carolina in recent years is when poet Patricia Hooper moved here from her native Michigan. She and her husband John settled in Gastonia, and Hooper, though she pined for significant snowfalls, continued writing her magnificent poems—quiet poems, stealthy poems, poems of shimmering insight and intelligence. Now the Tampa Review & Tampa Press announce that Hooper has won the Anita Claire Scharf Award for her fifth collection, "Separate Flights," to be published in 2016. The prize selects one book each year that "speaks to aspects of the journal's mission to praise and celebrate the beauty and diversity of the natural world; to illuminate the interconnectedness of our global environment; and to affirm the interrelatedness of visual and verbal art." Richard Matthews, editor of Tampa Review, said that Patricia Hooper's collection quite literally "lifts off." And he went on: "This brilliant and lyrical manuscript uses metaphors of flight—including birds and planes and arts—to explore and express the larger vision."

"Separate Flights" is Hooper's fourth full-length collection. Individual poems have appeared in The Atlantic Monthly, The American Scholar, Poetry, Ploughshares, The Southern Review and The Kenyon Review. She is also the author of four children's books.

[The Editor thanks Dannye Romine Powell for permission to reprint this *Charlotte Observer* review].

ROSMARIE WALDROP

Hopwood Award: 1963

Email to Donald Beagle

Did your Hopwood award impact your approach to subsequent work?

The Hopwood Award was extremely important for me. It gave me confidence that I could indeed write poetry in English, which is my second language. Laura Riding's biographer says poetry offered the immigrant's daughter a "refuge where the fear of speaking in strange ways could be left behind." This might have been a factor when I started writing in English. Poetry being itself a "foreign language"—at least this is what Proust said—it can be a home for interlopers like me. I very much appreciated Charles Tomlinson's thoughtful comments. They helped me see my strengths and weaknesses.

My personal life also owes much to the Award. I had met Keith Waldrop in Germany, and we had spent a year together studying in Aix-en-Provence. But only when he won the award in 1958 did we have the money for me to follow him to the US.

Andrea Beauchamp once said that Hopwood winners seem to fall into two groups when they re-read their student manuscripts: pleasantly surprised, or unpleasantly disappointed.

Some poems made it into my first book, but I soon moved on to other modes.

Which poets have influenced your own approach to writing poetry—ranging from "classics" to any contemporaries who may have influenced your mature work? Also, did any so-called "schools" of poetry impress you? Third, are you aware of (or care to share) any non-literary influences that have been especially important to your writing: music, visual art, social change, environmentalism, etc.?

Everything I read (and that engages me) "influences," or, rather, nourishes me. But here are some names. First Rilke, Gottfried Benn, Rimbaud, Mallarmé, Pound. Then the Vienna Group (especially Ersnt Jandl and Friederike Mayröcker), Robert Creeley, Gertrude Stein, Mina Loy, the Objectivists. John Cage. John Ashbery and Barbara Guest. And the French poets Anne-Marie Albiach, Claude Royet-Journoud, Jacques Roubaud, Emmanuel Hocquard, Edmond Jabès.

The Objectivists were the first "school" I read and embraced as a school. More recently I have felt very close to the LANGUAGE School.

Music has always been extremely important to me. And performance of the adventurous "avant garde" kind, e.g. by the Once Group, Fluxus, John Cage, Merce Cunningham. Also, Wittgenstein has informed much of my writing.

I went from very short lines, in which the object tumbles into being the subject of the next clause (two pairs of eyes/ see/ two different initial/ questions too/ disappear...) to writing novels. This gave me a more spacious sense of rhythm and led to my writing mostly prose poems afterwards.

Have you found poetry readings to be useful or enjoyable? Have you been at all attracted to, or intrigued by, the option of sharing poetry (or musings about poetry) online via social media or similar digital venues?

Poetry readings are great sounding boards. I like to read new work because they make me discover things that I missed when reading just by myself (including booboos!) And I value the social side, getting to meet other poets.

I don't do social media. E-mail alone is already taking up too much of my time.

Do you see modern academia in general as a good professional base for working poets? Do you feel the role of the poet in the academy has had any discernible impact—positive or negative—upon poetry in general?

Poets have to have jobs —we can't live by our writing. In France and Germany there are poet jobs in publishing, on the radio and TV. Here, aside from publishing houses, academe seems the only opportunity for a job that is germane to our work.

I'm not good at assessing impact. MFA programs have been much reviled and no doubt produce much dullness, but they certainly help young poets–whether by teaching craft, making writing-time available, or by showing what to rebel against

Here, I'd like to offer each poet the option of posing a question to yourself that perhaps you've never been asked, or wish you had been asked.

Of all my other activities, translating is the most rewarding. It has allowed me to "write" texts I could never have written on my own. I also has changed, "enlarged" my thinking considerably. The space between two languages demonstrates so clearly that nothing in language —or life —is ever one-dimensional, true/false, "cut-and-dried;" that there different perspectives on everything; that there remains an irreducible difference not only between languages but also between people which we do well to try to explore.

[**Editor's Note**: Quotes about Rosmarie Waldrop's Poetics]

"I don't even have thoughts, I say, I have methods that make language think, take over and me by the hand. Into sense or offense, syntax stretched across rules, relations of force, fluid the dip of the plumb line, the pull of eyes. What if the mother didn't censor the child's looking? Didn't wipe the slate clean? Would the child know from the start that there are no white pages, that we always write over a text already there? No beginnings. All unrepentant middle." – Rosmarie Waldrop; *A Form of Taking It All*; as quoted in: *The Poethical Wager*. Joan Retallack. (Berkeley : University of California Press, ©2003).

[This excerpt of 84 words is reproduced here under provision of Academic Fair Use.]

"A sequence of fragments seems the most appropriate form for a work of this kind, introductory, surveying, essentially personal, marked, as with all things, by my own reading and preoccupations. 'Maybe, ' Waldrop writes, 'the essence of the fragment is that it cuts out explanation, an essential act of poetry.' It constitutes, Waldrop continues, a 'lessening of distinctness, of "identity."' I do not claim to be comprehensive. Nor do I mean to speak for Waldrop or her work but simply to speak about some of its aspects, its various senses of poetics, the shifting relationships between theory and practice, to draw out a number of examples and to trace certain lines of thinking, ways of thinking." Quoted from: Nikolai Duffy; *Relative strangeness : reading Rosmarie Waldrop* [Bristol : Shearsman Books, 2013.]

[This excerpt of 116 words is reproduced here under provision of Academic Fair Use.]

"Rosmarie Waldrop has not only enjoyed three decades prominence as an American experimental poet but who has also actively promoted avant garde literature as a publisher (Burning Deck Press), as a teacher

(Brown University), and as a translator (Elke Erbe, Helmut Heissenbutttel, Edmond Jabes, and many other post-World War II Continental writers.) Moreover, a German immigrant to the United States, Waldrop has proved throughout her career to be exceptionally sensitive to the displacements, imbalances, and transpositions instigated by movement between nations, cultures, and languages. Her poetry is resolutely hybrid—"between," as she would say—as well as thoroughly secular and skeptical, preferring wit to ecstasy, insight to murkiness, and precision to evocative vagueness. An inquiry into Waldrop's compositional practice exposes the degree to which American innovative writing remains implicated in the trans-Atlantic crossing, collisions, and dispossessions that mark and mar so much of the country's past. Waldrop seeks through her writing a means of dwelling creatively, sustainingly in this chaotic, contested terrain." Quoted from: "Rosmarie Waldrop Renews Collage;" in: *Phenomenal Reading: Essays on Modern and Contemporary Poetics*. By Brian M. Reed. [University of Alabama Press, 2012].

[This excerpt of 162 words is reproduced here under provision of Academic Fair Use.]

"…Waldrop's poetry questions the persuasive clarity of visualization, and her poetry explores the gap between 'vague perceptual space and the precise space of visualization' or 'vague visual pictures.' Waldrop's poetry can cue us to our confidence in visual clarity and sharpen our sense of the difference between the logical rather than the physical congruence of our lives and language. Waldrop's poetry reflects the problem of visualizing the past by offering a vital alternative to representation that, too often, slips to formulaic narrative structures fooling us with a clarity derived from conventional order. Again, the importance of Waldrop's poetry includes how we might explore pictorial elements or procedure, and come to understand and critique how we learn conventions that shape how we see landscape, hear history, feel common sense, or imagine characters." Quoted from:

Deborah Meadows. "Reading Rosmarie Waldrop and Yoel Hoffmann: Embodied Thought and Linguistic Gap." *Another Language: Poetic Experiments in Britain and North America*; edited by Kornelia Freitag, Katharina Vester. [LIT Verlag Münster, 2008]

[This excerpt of 131 words is reproduced here under provision of Academic Fair Use.]

TOM CLARK

Hopwood Award: 1963

[**Editor's Note**: For nearly a decade, 2009-2018, poet Tom Clark maintained a densely-packed and richly-textured blog, titled *Tom Clark Beyond the Pale*. Here, he posted improvisations, reflections, scraps of poems by himself and others, complete poems from poets he liked and admired, reviews and commentaries on news of the day, and thousands of photographs drawn from a broad range of media.

Clark also accepted comments from readers, and frequently posted replies that rival his original blog posts in interest. Tom Clark never emailed me in response to my invitation to contribute. But in early August, long after I had given up, he did call my office—using a borrowed cellphone, he said—to ask after my progress. In that all-too-brief conversation, he said that if I really wished to include him "among the storied greats," as he jokingly put it, I was welcome to "harvest" some excerpts and selections from his blog.

He also kindly pointed me to a few specific posts he thought might be of special interest, such as his post on the Hopwood Awards and Frank O'Hara from December 2012. In a sense, Tom Clark's blog became a sort of 21st century counterpoint to John Ciardi's columns from *The Saturday Review*.

The following selections only hint at the fascinating range of this poet's enthusiasms, interests, and laments.

The last blog post excerpted here was dated August 13, 2018; Clark was killed in a traffic accident on August 18, 2018. He was 77.]

Excerpted Posts & Comments from *Beyond the Pale*, A Blog by Tom Clark

There Are Still Not Enough Stars: John Keats and Lyra (The Lyre)
WEDNESDAY, 25 FEBRUARY 2009

The whole fate drama hoving into view
Before dawn under the lyric stars...

Young Master Keats was an ostler's son born within earshot of Bow Bells. This tiny Cockney lad bore the social mark of the stables upon him, and the brand of class so deeply habituated into his speech that he would, as he rose in the world, take to self-mockingly imitating his own social awkwardness by abbreviating his name to "Junkets" when in the relaxed company of certain friends. Yet he determined early on—despite the enormity of the ambition, considering his mean class status—to make a name for himself in time to come as among "the English Poets."

At play among the minor magnitudes as a child
Above the Swan and Hoop Keats toys with stars,

Sky bodies dance like tops in agile
Imaginings of his small street boxer's hands.
Rising over London Wall, anchoring the Summer Triangle,
Vega, a bluish white star of major magnitude in Lyra,
Is conspicuous in its passage from the south
Over the smoky fogbound eighteenth century town.

We hear in the Mythologies John Keats read at school—the "light classics" versions of Greek and Latin poets' tales, providing an underprivileged child's tenuous grasp upon infinitely desirable "Realms of Gold"—that Hermes found an empty tortoise shell on the beach and strung seven strings through the holes, and that light shimmered then upon the strings, which when plucked delivered heavenly sounds.

Losing himself into the moment of his studenthood,
Prosing the Aeneid, learning Lemprière by heart,
Scanning, while downstairs Cowden Clarke practised Mozart,
The night sky anatomy of a mythic

Pre-world with its promise of high morning heroism and its
Even higher paradigms of expanding darkness—
Already by some poet instinct knowing that here in the universe
The evening is young, there are still not enough stars…

Hermes swapped this instrument to Apollo for a magic healing staff entwined with snakes. The staff also possessed the ability to render its owner airborne. But Apollo did not feel cheated in the exchange, for he now possessed the divine power of song.

Apollo passed on the power of song to his son, Orpheus, but not without warning him about the special concealed defect of this wonderful gift. Though it was a very strong power, it left you in many ways defenseless, because you could not do harm with it. And the defect concealed in this gift? You might well die for the possessing of it….

All through that aching starlit spring
In Hampstead..

At a literal and historical level, the astronomical Lyra is a sky-sign under which Keats was born. In his life story the poet's lyre appears as a figure of poetic gift—meanwhile also distantly beckoning overhead, through the smoke and gaslight and fog, as that remote constellation in the London night sky.

After a night of whisk and brag and gin and water
At Rice's cardplaying club on Poland Street,
Coming out before dawn under the lyric stars,
Vega conspicuous at the point of the Lyre

At five o'clock of a summer morning encompassing
286 degrees of the London Arabic sky,

The whole fate drama hoving into view,
While the slow making of souls overshadows

Every thing...

Frank O'Hara: *Les Étiquettes Jaunes*
SATURDAY, 22 DECEMBER 2012

This poem comes from Frank's Hopwood manuscript, compiled in a roominghouse in Ann Arbor during the winter of 1950-1951. The Avery Hopwood awards offered a tiny cash enticement to writers at a time when the entire idea of "creative writing" (and of cash prizes for its accomplishment) still lay blissfully unhatched, as when the Alien lay slumbering in its subterranean pod. The cash prize a small withered carrot dangling from the end of the short sharp stick of a harsh frostbound Ann Arbor winter. A few years later the same dubious enticement drew me also. A few years later still —by now Frank was dead, run down at 39 by a dune buggy on Fire Island — I visited Ann Arbor in the winter permafrost with Ted Berrigan, who insisted on being ushered to the sacred site of Frank's temporary residence.

We labored up the hill through the hard ungiving elements, nostrils frozen together, small puffs of breath poking the frigid air out ahead of us, Ted growing less committed to the quest with each tentative step into the deep snow covering what was assumed to be sidewalk. We arrived, had a look — an ordinary drab Midwestern roominghouse, no distinguishing features. The last leaf of autumn long since withered and gone:

> I picked up a leaf
> today from the sidewalk.
> This seems childish.
>
> Leaf! you are so big!
> How can you change your
> color, then just fall!
>
> As if there were no
> such thing as integrity!
>
> You are too relaxed
> to answer me. I am too
> frightened to insist.
>
> Leaf! don't be neurotic
> like the small chameleon.

Frank O'Hara: *Les Étiquettes Jaunes*, Ann Arbor, September 1950, from *Meditations in an Emergency*, 1957

[following: excerpted replies to comments]

Thanks all, on a day more than full of winter it is gladdening to hear I am not alone in seeing this poem as a small herald to hark the arrival of a genius. Particularly the tonal command, the trick of assimilating and incorporating a certain French style into the unique American wit — and the delicate, only half-ironic wistfulness, and the romance, and of course the sense of humour.

In lines 7-8, the mastery is already evident. And in the poem of an M.A. candidate, yet! (Ann Arbor does have its autumnal beauties, before the ice storms set in.)

….Phil's [Larkin] observation about Frank having Hart Crane's eyes is indeed arresting. (One recalls "The Eyes of Laura Mars".)

And of course Phil and Frank did see eye to eye on many things.

And re. the Hopwoods— over the infinite years there have obviously been many (if not myriad) winners in the various categories. The Hopwood website keeps the whole list updated, I believe, if you can bother to fiddle with the requisite PDF'ing.

Wiki lists these selected recipients:

Brett Ellen Block, Max Apple, Lorna Beers, Sven Birkerts, John Malcolm Brinnin, John Ciardi, Tom Clark, Lyn Coffin, Cid Corman, Christopher Paul Curtis, Mary Gaitskill, Robert Hayden, Garrett Hongo, Lawrence Joseph, Jane Kenyon, Laura Kasischke, Elizabeth Kostova, Arthur Miller, Howard Moss, Davi Napoleon, Frank O'Hara, Marge Piercy, William Craig Rice, Ari Roth, Davy Rothbart, Betty Smith, Ron Sproat, Keith Waldrop, Rosmarie Waldrop, Edmund White, Nancy Willard, Beth Tanenhaus Winsten, and Maritta Wolff.

Of those, Max Apple was my classmate... and the Waldrops were also on the scene, with their own basement hand press.

Yes and Oh for the bright unapologetic times and tones evoked by the memoria of all that gone joy and gladness (not to mention the gentle pre-technological sadness), buried now under the endless snows of yesteryear, upon which cascade the black deluges of right now.

All my sad old man's clothes draped over a rickety plastic drying rack, dripping with the bathos.

Kent, My landlord on E. Ann St. in A2, had inherited and helpfully passed along lurid family tales concerning epic filial trauma skeletons rattling in the Roethke greenhouse closet, and these were compounded by the then current academic poet gossip concerning Teddy's amazing then-present-tense bad behaviour, reportedly permitted, even indeed possibly egged-on, by his astonishingly broadminded depot chair at U-Dub, so that...

How many of those weird memories could it take to squeeze under one sweater at the soda fountain counter at Schwab's?

But nothing is sacred any more, especially not the great cultural myths.

Academic poetry then and now, enough to cause one to wish to dive under that capacious sweater and never again come out...

(When quizzed on what he'd learned at the 75th(?) Anniversary Hopwood by-invite-only dinner, author and past Hoppy winner Bruce Shlain replied, [....]

"Lana Turner never did win that Hopwood, although she was discovered at Schwab's drugstore by Theodore Roethke, who was wearing the same sweater.")

Against that background, then, Frank, staying on his feet even when the deck pitched... until he didn't:

> Poem [Lana Turner has Collapsed!]
>
> Lana Turner has collapsed!
> I was trotting along and suddenly
> it started raining and snowing
> and you said it was hailing
> but hailing hits you on the head
> hard so it was really snowing and
> raining and I was in such a hurry

to meet you but the traffic
was acting exactly like the sky
and suddenly I see a headline
LANA TURNER HAS COLLAPSED!
there is no snow in Hollywood
there is no rain in California
I have been to lots of parties
and acted perfectly disgraceful
but I never actually collapsed
oh Lana Turner we love you get up

Frank O'Hara (1926-1966): *Poem [Lana Turner has Collapsed!]*, from *Lunch Poems*,
(The Old Masters, they were always wrong about the rain in California.)

Richard Brautigan: Lonely at the Laundromat
THURSDAY, 20 FEBRUARY 2014

This poem was found written on a paper bag by Richard Brautigan in a laundromat in San Francisco. The author is unknown.

By accident, you put
Your money in my
Machine (#4)
By accident, I put
My money in another
Machine (#6)
On purpose, I put
Your clothes in the
Empty machine full
Of water and no
Clothes
It was lonely.

Richard Brautigan (1935-1984): *San Francisco,* from *All Watched Over by Machines of Loving Grace,* 1967

[excerpted from replies to comments]

Thanks, all. Good to dwell among the loyal. Reconsidering Richard and his work, a bittersweet contemplation, yet instructive in many ways. We're reminded that the trade winds shift with the times; and that great short-term celebrity, seemingly the immediate desideratum of every start-out writer in these days post the death of modesty, can do more harm than good in many cases, especially once the descent from the heights begins, and the taste of aloes and the score-settling set in.

Richard's stated and quite touching specific stipulation for this and the other poems in this small book put out by The Communications Company in 1967, by the way, was that the work might be used by anyone for anything, so long as profit wasn't involved.

Just imagine that. So you'll understand, it was a different kind of time.

Laundromats are forlorn places even if you're not locked in overnight.

As recently as a few years back, when still ambulatory, I often sought shelter from the storms in a late-night laundromat, where one might meditate indefinitely (well, until eleven). And there, with the attendant absent and the place empty, one found oneself surrounded by stray articles of clothing, sad abandoned and lost, most typically socks separated from their partners, or whatever the other half of a pair is called.

Wallace Stevens: Thinking of a Relation between the Images of Metaphors
FRIDAY, 29 MAY 2015

Thinking of a Relation is one of several poems in *Transport to Summer* that consciously evoke the poet's origins and early life in eastern Pennsylvania, where he was belatedly locating a central site of autobiographical reminiscence and reflection. In the construction of a poetic mythos, this landscape, at once experienced and endeared, became fantastic, loomed over by shadows, sometimes "shadows of friends" ("A Completely New Set of Objects"), sometimes shadows more ominous — here, unseen but imagined figures "upstream", round the next bend of the Perkiomen, representing the now absent "Indians", whose "waterish spears" are still feared by the ahistorical bass in the creek.

"Neshaminy is a little place seven or eight miles from Doylestown," Stevens wrote to genealogist Lila James Roney on 2 November 1942, naming a small Pennsylvania community that was for him the locus of a now half-imaginal personal/paternal/pastoral arcadia recalled from boyhood. "To the west of it lies the country through which the Perkiomen Creek flows. This creek, when I was a boy was famous for its bass. It almost amounts to a genealogical fact that all his life long my father used to fish in [the Perkiomen], and this can only mean that he did it as a boy."

Stevens came from Holland Dutch stock; his native region had a strong Moravian Dutch presence. Over time, under British colonial influence and thereafter, the native Lenape people of the region—the departed but not-forgot-by-the-bass "Indians"—were "removed" to the west; they are remembered now only in place-names, many of which are inscribed in Stevens' poems of this period.

Perkiomen Creek is a 37.7-mile-long (60.7 km.) tributary of the Schuylkill River in Berks, Lehigh and Montgomery counties, Pennsylvania.

The name Perkiomen derives from the Lenape term Pakhim Unk [Pah-Keym-Unk] — in English, "cranberry place".

A historical scholar has held up the "removal" of the Lenape of the North American Middle Atlantic as a paradigmatic instance of the progress of Western imperialism in the age of expansion:

The wood-doves are singing along the Perkiomen.
The bass lie deep, still afraid of the Indians.

In the one ear of the fisherman, who is all
One ear, the wood-doves are singing a single song.

The bass keep looking ahead, upstream, in one
Direction, shrinking from the spit and splash

Of waterish spears. The fisherman is all
One eye, in which the dove resembles a dove.

There is one dove, one bass, one fisherman.
Yet coo becomes rou-coo, rou-coo. How close

To the unstated theme each variation comes . . .
In that one ear it might strike perfectly:

State the disclosure. In that one eye the dove
Might spring to sight and yet remain a dove.

The fisherman might be the single man
In whose breast, the dove, alighting, would grow still.

Wallace Stevens (1879-1955): *Thinking of a Relation between the Images of Metaphors*, from *Transport to Summer*, 1947

Sacrifice | illusionary lives | backfire
MONDAY, 13 AUGUST 2018

On Ed Dorn & Mayan Translations

Having no Spanish nor any way back into the literatures and visual languages of the prior inhabitants of the Americas without intelligent assistance, Ed was fortunate to find a willing and able guide in the British scholar Gordon Brotherston, a mutual friend who was our colleague at Essex; with Gordon's essential help, a number of Mesoamerican and Native American texts were English'd. Hieroglyphic picture languages having fascinated Ed's teacher Charley O, likewise himself devoid of necessary skills in the field, this was by the 1960s proving a fruitful area of pursuit for anyone who had taken seriously the work of everybody's Master Ez P who spent a lifetime in tireless search of a visual language transferable to the page; an impatience with the blind tunnels of the "western" way of the Logos (or anyway its historical misuse as doctrinal authority) was the common impetus in all these efforts. What they had in common was a dim or maybe sometimes clearer inkling of the historical truth, that the Europeans who had come to and conquered the "New World"— new and promising of course, to them, as any wondrously abundant new place was always going to be, to the Colonial Mind. How to advantageously short circuit that Mind while also retaining privileged access and ultimately dominant entitlement to the entire hemisphere, continually extracting and exploiting its great natural wealth and resources and subjugating as convenient cheap labour and finally killing off those of the native peoples who got in the way of the project— obviously that grandly ambitious clean-up operation, riddled with contradiction and aporia as it is, goes on down to this day. However one does fear it is only disingenuous at best, patronizing at worst to pretend a belated concern for what has been so purposefully destroyed over such a long period in such a callous, disrespectful, wasteful and cruel fashion.

This patch of the hemisphere we're on now is going up in smoke, all the best of it wafting down as polluting particulate, and I reckon no Ohlone native with a very long memory would know what to make of it. The Redding fire which killed ten and decimated a forest was sparked by something so little-big as a trailer hitch dragging on hot asphalt ("our way of life"). Pouring molten gold down the throats of the cutthroat commuters ramming their poisonous shitmobiles up and down the freeway feeder in quest of goods or money or fun or combinations of the above, at this moment, sounds a fine idea "in theory"— but in actual practice, battling the insane windmill-whirly traffic defensively (quixotically!) with my medicare-dispensed cane, far less effective, if less costly.

And you know the pavements would soon enough be cluttered with opportunistic techies who arrived here last week, scraping up the precious metal residue with a Mind to Doing a Deal.

Don't know if the news has escaped these shores, but didjew know that Herr Drumpf, upon swearing in as Boss of Murica, requested that the Book upon which he be sworn be not the Bible but...

The Art of the Deal.

Then, it was still possible to say No to him.

Posted 13 AUGUST 2018

[Tom Clark died on August 18, 2018.]

LAWRENCE JOSEPH

Hopwood Award: 1970

Email to Donald Beagle

I graduated from Detroit's Jesuit high school—the University of Detroit High School—in June 1966, and started at Michigan that fall. I wrote my first poems in Ann Arbor—my freshman year, in early '67. I can't remember precisely when, but it must have been during my freshman year that I first heard of the Hopwood Awards and their prestigious history. I was in Honors English; during my junior and senior years I took survey courses in English Literature and literary criticism from Chaucer to the present, and in my junior year I also took courses from Donald Hall on Pound, Yeats, and Joyce. In the summer of '69, I was accepted into Donald Hall's upper-level poetry creative writing course for the fall, which was limited in size and to seniors and graduate students only. That summer I also went to London for the first time, and discovered books in translation in the Penguin Modern European Poets series, many of which were not available in the United States (and which I still have). During that fall and early winter I wrote all but two or three of the poems included in my Hopwood manuscript. The title I chose for the manuscript—*18 Poems*—was the same title as Dylan Thomas's first collection, which was published shortly before his twentieth birthday. I had the option, at the time, to submit poems for either a minor or major Hopwood (graduate students could only submit for a major award). I submitted my manuscript for a major award, which I received in late February or early March of my last semester. Robert Bly and X.J. Kennedy (a former Hopwood winner) were the judges.

The award had an inestimable impact on me. It most of all confirmed a decision I'd already felt compelled to make, to commit my life to seriously writing poetry. It also reinforced my decision to go to graduate school in English (I'd received a two-year fellowship to study English Literature at Magdalene College, the University of Cambridge, sponsored by the Power Foundation). Lawrence Kasdan, whom I'd met through friends the previous fall while studying for a Physiology exam—we were introduced to each other as "writers"—also won a major award that year in Drama for "Just-This: A Feature-Length Screenplay," and Max Apple—later to become a close friend—won three Major awards, in Essay, Fiction (Novel), and Fiction (Short Story); Nadine Gordimer delivered the Hopwood Lecture. Shortly after receiving the award, I met Robert Hayden at a Phi Beta Kappa dinner for graduating seniors. Hayden—who received a post-graduate degree from Michigan and received two major Hopwood awards—joined the Michigan faculty in the fall of '69. We were introduced to each other first of all as fellow Hopwood winners.

I returned from England in late '72 and began law school at Michigan in the summer of '73. Several of my professors in law school were aware of my Hopwood award, and its prominence at Michigan. I kept very much in touch with poets and writers in Ann Arbor at the time, and visited the Hopwood Room several times a week. In 1981, Harry Thomas (a Hopwood winner) and Steven Lavine—both of whom later became good friends—edited *The Hopwood Anthology: Five Decades of American Poetry*, published by the University of Michigan Press. It included "When You've Been Here Long Enough," a poem later published in my first book *Shouting at No One*. It was the first time a poem of mine was anthologized. In May 1991, The Writer's Voice of the West Side YMCA in New York City sponsored an evening of readings at the Ethical Cultural Auditorium in honor of the *Michigan Quarterly Review*. Larry Goldstein, the *MQR*'s editor, presented the event. I read with Charles Baxter and Diane Ackerman, and former Hopwood winners Marge Piercy and Arthur Miller. It was especially meaningful for me to meet and read with Marge Piercy, also from Detroit, and recipient of Hopwood awards in both poetry and fiction, and Arthur Miller, who chose to attend Michigan because of the Hopwood awards, and whose appreciation of his Hopwood award was pronounced, lifelong, and profound.

The poems in my Hopwood manuscript are primarily drawn from the work of poets I was reading at the time. There are two or three strongly imagistic poems, influenced by Pound's early poems and Waley's and Rexroth's translations from the Chinese. There are also poems modeled after three poets in the Penguin Modern European Poets series: the Yugoslavian poet Vasko Popa, the Czech poet Miroslav Holub, and the Polish poet Zbigniew Herbert. There are poems with mythical and classical allusions, and poems with liturgical, psalm-like language. I also was closely reading, studying, W.S. Merwin's *The Lice*. The final poem in the manuscript, "Mythistorema," is in several parts. The title is from a poem by the Greek poet George Seferis; its parts of are patterned mostly after poems by Seferis—in Edmund Keeley's and Philip Sherrard's translations—and a poem by the Chilean poet Nicanor Parra , "What the Deceased Had to Say About Himself," translated by Thomas Merton. One part of "Mythistorema" opens with the line "I was appointed the poet of heaven." In early 1971, it was published in *Varsity*, a Cambridge, England literary magazine, whose poetry editor, David Lehman, I met shortly after coming to study at the University of Cambridge in the fall of 1970 (David was a Kellett Fellow at Clare College). I told David that the poem was part of a Hopwood award manuscript—he knew of the award because Frank O'Hara, as a graduate student at Michigan, received a Hopwood. I later changed the poem's last line, and placed the poem, in italics, as the prologue poem to *Shouting at No One*. It's the only poem from *18 Poems* that I've published in a book:

I was appointed the poet of heaven.

It was my duty to describe
Theresa's small roses
as they bent in the wind.

I tired of this
and asked you to let me
write about something else.
You ordered, "Sit
in the trees where the angels sleep
and copy their breaths
in verse.

So I did,
and soon I had a public following:

Saint Agnes with red cheeks,
Saint Dorothy with a moon between her fingers
and the Hosts of Heaven.

You said, "You've failed me."
I told you, "I'll write lovelier poems,"
but, you answered,
"You've already had your chance:

you will be pulled from a womb
into a city."

The city the poet of heaven is pulled into is the Detroit that emotionally dominates the physical and metaphorical landscapes of the poems in *Shouting at No One*.

While I was in Cambridge, I decided not to pursue further graduate studies in English, or to attend one of the few graduate creative writing programs that existed then, but, instead, to return to Ann Arbor to study law. It was a choice made for a number of reasons—one of which was the fact that I come from a lower-middle-working class background and I feared, correctly, in the very tight academic market at the time, having to make my living in the economically uncertain worlds of English Literature or Creative Writing. As for how I would make my living and write poetry, I very much had in mind the examples of Wallace Stevens, a surety-bond lawyer, and Williams Carlos Williams, a doctor, who, in their time, chose to make their livings outside prevailing literary and academic circles. I've had a professional career as a lawyer for over forty years—as a judicial law clerk, a practicing litigator, and, mostly, as a law professor and legal scholar. I've made poems now for over fifty-years, which I make basically the same way that I made the poems in *18 Poems*—in effect, creating my own tradition, an ongoing process that is never static , constantly evolving. In a recent interview in the *Michigan Quarterly Review* with Phillip Metres, I describe my tradition as encompassing the work of poets of great formal power and compositional skill; poets who write out of a moral witness that brings into focus political power-structures, racism, misogyny, the destruction of labor, the destruction of the environment, the vicious hatred of the poor and weak, the systemic corporate-statist violence that underlies imperial war-making; poets who employ intimate, sensual language, languages of beauty and love, of color and light; poets who write almost entirely out of the language of their interior worlds. Metres asks: "In many respects, your new book, *So Where Are We?* feels like a continuation of *Into It*, which continued from *Before Our Eyes*. Is this progression your sense of the books too?" I answer: "It is—and *Before Our Eyes* is a continuation of *Curriculum Vitae*, and *Curriculum Vitae* of *Shouting at No One*. I am among those poets—Wallace Stevens, Eugenio Montale, Louis Zukofsky, and, crucially, Adrienne Rich, also among them—who see themselves writing one long poem."

I've often said, in interviews and at readings, that the first poem in my first book—the first poem of my one long poem—is "I was appointed the poet of heaven," which, I add, I wrote my senior year at Michigan shortly before my twenty-second birthday, and which, I proudly say, is part of a manuscript of poems that received a Hopwood major award.

LAWRENCE JOSEPH

Born in Detroit in 1948 and the grandson of Syrian Lebanese immigrants, Lawrence Joseph was educated at the University of Michigan (B.A. 1970), the University of Cambridge (M.A. 1972), and the University of Michigan Law School (J.D. 1975). He is the author of six books of poetry—*So Where Are We?* (2017); *Into It* (2005); *Codes, Precepts, Biases, and Taboos: Poems 1973–1993* (2005), which includes *Before Our Eyes* (1993), *Curriculum Vitae* (1988), and *Shouting at No One* (1983)—published by Farrar, Straus and Giroux. He is also the author of *Lawyerland* (1997), a nonfiction novel, also published by FSG, and *The Game Changed: Essays and Other Prose* (2011), which appears in the University of Michigan Press's Poets on Poetry series. His *Selected Poems* is forthcoming with FSG. His work is widely anthologized, and has been translated into several languages. Among his awards are fellowships from the Guggenheim Foundation and the National Endowment for the Arts. He is Tinnelly Professor of Law at St. John's University School of Law and lives New York City.

JANE KENYON

Hopwood Award: 1970

[**Editor's Note:** I never met Jane Kenyon. My most memorable meeting with her husband, Donald Hall, came by way of a guest seminar he conducted for a poetry workshop run by Harriet Stolorow. Stolorow won a Hopwood Award herself as a Masters Degree candidate in 1968, and had begun teaching at Jackson Community College by 1970, when Kenyon won her own award. Soon after, Jane agreed to sit down with Harriet for a conversation.

Harriet later shared with me her transcription and interpretive notes, commenting that she saw Jane Kenyon as one of the most promising young poets on the Ann Arbor scene. She also made me promise confidentiality; otherwise I would simply reprint that transcription here.

Donald Hall's death during this book's preparation did prompt me to scan the literature on Kenyon to see how well Stolorow's early insights held up (e.g.; her thoughts on Kenyon's bouts with depression; her perspective on the poet's "…courageous probing of existential darkness for glimmers of enlightenment." My literature review led to this article by Australian poet Rose Lucas.

I want to thank Rose Lucas for granting me permission to reprint "Into Black Air." I admire the multiple ways it brings Stolorow's conversation with Kenyon to a sort of fulfillment through its own estimable insights.]

"Into black air":
Darkness and its Possibilities in the Poetry of Jane Kenyon

By Rose Lucas

> If it's darkness
> we're having, let it be extravagant.[6]

The poetic lyric in free verse form, as Kenyon used it, is imagistically and structurally compressed, often with a final volta or twist, and pivots on the crucial intersection between the subjective voice and the field of external perceptions. As a distillation of poetic structure in general, the lyric's structural and emotional focus on the centrality of the image and its metaphoric possibilities[7] makes it able to operate at a nexus between a subjective interior and an exteriorized articulation; it is this which provides Kenyon with the perceptual and communicative scaffolding with which to understand and accommodate an experience of life as inevitably fractured with loss, grief and even clinical depression. In a poem to her dying father, she describes life, rather than death, as the period of exile which is to be endured:

> This is the abyss.
> That's why babies howl at birth,
> and why the dying so often reach
> for something only they can apprehend.
> ("Reading Aloud to My Father," CP, 291)

---

[6] Jane Kenyon, "Taking Down the Tree" (1990), in *Collected Poems*. (Saint Paul, Minnesota: Graywolf Press, 2005), 153. Hereafter abbreviated as *CP*.

[7] See for examples Kenyon's introduction to her translations of "Twenty Poems of Anna Akhmatova" (1985), and her assertion there that "Image embodies feeling, and this embodiment is perhaps the greatest treasure of lyric poetry." Reprinted in *A Hundred White Daffodils: Essays, Interviews, The Akhmatova Translations, Newspaper Columns and One Poem*, (Saint Paul, Minnesota: Graywolf Press, 1999), 7.

Kenyon's poetic does not shy away from any delineations of such an abyss and is at times confronting in its depictions of the bleakness of those holes in the fabric of a life through which one can fall—into the suffocating grip of what she refers to as "the anti-urge,/the mutilator of souls" ("Having It Out With Melancholy," *CP*, 231). Indeed, the poetic act, so hard won, will not always be successful in its efforts to provide consolation for despair, or frameworks of meaning to apparent meaninglessness. As Kenyon notes in the small poem "Depression," language will not always be adequate to bridge the chasm between desire and its object, between despair and the far shores of faith. This poem itself is fractured with dusty ellipses, suggestive here not of a wealth of extra-linguistic possibilities but rather of the possibilities of failure and melancholic powerlessness; its descriptions beat hollow, desperate to summon up the power of a narrative of redemption, yet confronting the always-imminent failure to invoke that longed for presence:

> …a mote. A little world. Dusty. Dusty.
> The universe is dust. Who can bear it?
> Christ comes. The women feed him, bathe his feet
> with tears, bring spices, find the empty tomb,
> burst out to tell the men, are not believed …
> (CP, 93)

Nevertheless, in spite of, and perhaps even because of this dusty drag into melancholic despair with its failure to cohere fragments into any kind of story of redemption, Kenyon's is also a poetic which resolutely strives to affirm the possibility of a positively connoted "urge," to unearth and affirm the drive which brings, "like friends the green-white crowns/of perennials. They have the tender,/unnerving beauty of a baby's head" ("Ice Out," *CP*, 195). Her poetics document success and failure, dark as well as light—the drive of the desire for life, and for the sustenance of both body and spirit, as well as the death-bearing inertia which eschews even the power to speak. Evoking, describing, sometimes listing what Gwen Harwood has referred to as the "small voices" of the images.[8] precise and drawn from the world which surrounds us, Kenyon provides us with a scaffolding of poetic imagery which comforts, if not rescues us from the silence of loss—loss of loved ones; loss of one's agency; loss of faith in the very possibilities of continuity and redemption.

In these ways, I argue that Kenyon enacts a poetic labour of mourning, forging a poetics of tentative presence which nevertheless acknowledges the loss or lack which variously underpins human experience. Like all poets of mourning, she is actively concerned to trace, lovingly and in an often incantatory way, what is present and graspable as well as what is not, what can only be suggested through the agency of the metaphor. In Kenyon's poetry, this pulsing of possibility and loss, image and its shadow, is most recurringly evoked through images of darkness and light, particularly as they operate within the senses of the physical world. Such images and thematics abound throughout her poetry: *From Room to Room* (1978), *The Boat of Quiet Hours* (1986), *Let Evening Come* (1990), *Constance* (1993), and the *Collected Poems* (2005), published a decade after her early death from leukemia in 1995. Tracing a direct line both from the Romantics' interest in the figurative possibilities of the natural world, and also from an Imagist, or modernist, preoccupation with the pared down "natural image as the [always] adequate symbol,"[9]

Kenyon's poetic figures a play of light and dark, of hope, despair and the shadows of possibility—primarily by means of the precisely visualized and experienced imagery of the natural world, in particular

---

[8] See Gwen Harwood's description: "until we learn to listen/to small voices that tell/in fennel-plume, grass tassel,/the mystery of renewal/in ripening change," "Tetragrammaton," *Collected Poems 1943–1995*, ed. Gregory Kratzamann and Alison Hoddinott (St Lucia: University of Queensland Press, 2003), 436.

[9] Kenyon herself cited and adopted Ezra Pound's famous dictum of his Imagist manifesto that the "natural object is always the adequate symbol," "Everything I Know About Writing Poetry (Notes for a Lecture)," in *A Hundred White Daffodils,* 140.

the world of her life with poet Donald Hall at Eagle Pond Farm in rural New Hampshire. As the critic Robert Spirko notes, Kenyon's poetry offers a crucial "confluence of experience and emotion, the place where the objective and the subjective come together."[10] The poetic perception of the external world—its objects, seasons, people, relationships—not only notices and describes that world, performing the vital task of drawing a reader's attention to the things outside the small house of themselves, but, in a manner reminiscent of Whitman's great inventories of detail and perception, focuses attention upon that point of confluence, where the self confronts the wild and open fields of alterity, where the individual voice of experience overlaps, albeit only momentarily, with the cosmos in which it recognizes itself. It is in the linguistic imaginary of such a confluence that the single voice is able to articulate interior perception through the language and the imagery of the visible world. Reflecting on her own role as poet, Kenyon theorized, "We feel this pressure of emotion and thought, and we need to find, among the many things of this world, a way to *body forth* our feeling. It's metaphor, the engine of poetry, that does the work for us."[11] Echoing here Williams' sense of the poem as a "machine made of words," as well as his insistence upon the poetic praxis which asserts that there can be "no ideas except in things,"[12] Kenyon highlights the emotional as well as the technical work required by the poem as a confluence of inside and outside: to "body forth" that interior world into landscapes of the recognizable; as well as representing that exteriority—the specificity of lichen, or hay bales, or peony flowers—inevitably through the lens of the subjective.

---

[10] Robert Spirko, "Affective Disorders: The Treatment of Emotion in Jane Kenyon's Poetry," in *'Bright Unequivocal Eye': Poems, Papers, and Remembrances from the First Jane Kenyon Conference*, ed. Bert G. Hornbeck (New York: Peter Lang, 2000), 122.
[11] Kenyon, "Everything I Know About Writing Poetry," in *A Hundred White Daffodils*, 139.
[12] William Carlos William, "Author's Introduction to *The Wedge* (1944)," *William Carlos Williams: Selected Essays* (New York: New Directions, 1954), 256; *Paterson*, Section 1 (Harmondsworth: Penguin, 1963), 6.

The seemingly simple early poem "For the Night" (*CP*, 5), raises this interplay of a complex imagery of light and dark which informs her entire poetic:

> The mare kicks
> in her darkening stall, knocks
> over a bucket.
>
> The goose...
>
> The cow keeps a peaceful brain
> behind her broad face.
>
> Last light moves
> through cracks in the wall,
> over bales of hay.
>
> And the bat lets
> go of the rafters, falls
> into black air.

On a literal level, the poem describes the attenuated movement of the day and its creatures into the night. Kenyon repeatedly returns to this shifting time of twilight as a literal and metaphoric site of transition and potential transformation. This has the effect of both highlighting the temporal nature of the world and its things, enacting the idea that while there may be cycles there are also inevitably limits and final closures—"but one day, I know,/it will be otherwise" as she writes of life and love and health in "Otherwise," *CP*, 266)—while also drawing attention to the symbolic significance of the two distinct spheres at their transformative point of intersection.

As this, and many other poems, makes clear, Kenyon does not present a dichotomised and unequivocal view of light/day as positive and dark/night as negative. Rather, the poems reflect the complex of associations and possibilities associated with each position. On one level, the falling night here could be understood as a lack or a failure of light, thereby casting the speaker into the exilic experience of darkness; in this sense, the poem might operate elegiacally, as a nostalgic grieving for a day which brings clarity, wakefulness, even usefulness. The kicking of the mare for example is, on one level, an incident of ordinariness, part of the fabric of the business of putting farm animals away at the end of a working day. However, it might also suggest something of Dylan Thomas' notion of "raging"[13]—here, perhaps as everywhere, ineffectually—at the loss of light and the life which is associated with it.

However, the poem is in fact dedicated "For the Night," and thus it also operates something like a gift to or token of appreciation for what it is the night might represent. Like any gift, it symbolizes an economy of giving, an exchange that is profoundly bi-directional. The night does not simply take away the blessings of the light—the productivity of the farm, the harvesting of the grasses as provision for the future—but offers something different, something *as well as*. The speaking voice takes its point of perception inside the contained space, inside the walls of the barn, watching, delineating, as "Last light moves/through cracks in the wall,/over bales of hay"; yet this movement of the light— natural, inevitable according to the logic of the physical world—is not simply evidence of the entropic passage of time and mortality. The point of perception is situated within the edifice of structure, even within the house of poetic language, but this is a house which is also open to the external world, significantly not sealed against the possibilities of change and loss. And as loss of one sort slowly takes place, as the "Last light moves," the space of the barn/the space of the

---

[13] Dylan Thomas, "Rage, rage against the dying of the light," from "Do not go gentle into that good night," in *Miscellany One: Poems, Stories, Broadcasts* (London: Dent, Everyman, 1963), 31.

poem becomes a sphere of change—a change that always has the potential for both fearfulness and the inspiration of what is unexpected, the not-self which can only come upon us in the hiatus of loss and uncertainty.

In an interview with Bill Moyers, and referring to another poem "The Bat" (*CP*, 114), in which the movement of the bat's wings is likened to the "third person/in the Trinity.../the one who astounded Mary/by suddenly coming near," Kenyon commented:

> What I had in mind was being broken in upon, the way Mary was broken in upon by Gabriel. You think you're alone and suddenly there's this thing coming near you, so near that you can feel the wind from the brushing of its wings.[14]

Similarly, in "For the Night," the final stanza brings not only an additional piece of physical description, but a sense of an otherness "breaking in upon" the space of the speaker. And where the previous elements of the poem focus upon the visible, the watching of the light and its effects, these last lines move us into another sphere—of sound, the sensed pressure of wing beats in air—taking us to a different, unpredictable place. The bat certainly carries some associations of gothic terror, emblematizing the possibility of a vampiric plunge which leaves the speaker, unprotected by light, vulnerable to time's assault upon the corporeal body. However, as Kenyon's references to the wings of the angel Gabriel suggest, there is also a strong evocation of a positive, even transformative and inspirational aspect of this encounter with night's messenger. Indeed, there is even a suggestion of identification of speaker with bat—an inhabiting of the metaphor of exteriority as a vehicle for a movement beyond the sphere of the known, the safe, the recognizable.

---

[14] Kenyon, "An Interview with Bill Moyers (1993)," in *A Hundred White Daffodils*, 165.

The bat "lets go" of the stability and shelter of the rafters, and its transition into the space of the barn/poem is figured as a "fall[ing]," a loss of control and agency that can either signify impending disaster or the emotional "free-fall" which Adrienne Rich [15] describes as an essential component for any movement out of stasis, a necessary step to ensure the possibility of new life—poetically, emotionally, psychically. Such a risky, yet potentially productive free-falling also evokes Williams' articulation of modernism's charge that any concept of the new is only possible through the dangerous collapsing of the old—"a flaw, a crack in the bowl" of preconception: "It is this that one means when he says destruction and creation are simultaneous."[16]

The poem suggests that to find the next (always new) experience or understanding, it is imperative to "let go" of the supporting and shielding rafters to fall into that black air, just as, in order to convey the imperative and the risk of that plunge, it is necessary to find a new poetic house in which to accommodate and articulate that experience. "What a lark! What a plunge!" feels Mrs. Dalloway at the beginning of Virginia Woolf's novel.[17] As that modernist literary experiment suggests, the "plunge" can be one both of inspiration, of courage and newness derived from that "breaking in upon" of alterity, as it also inevitably correlated, within the structures of that narrative, with the suicidal plunge of Septimus Smith over his balcony. The fall "into black air," where the night can be read both as a sea of inscriptive ink and of drowning, will thus always be one which encompasses an equivocation and an ambiguity of possibilities.

It is the plunge of poetic inspiration, the energy that moves and drives any kind of creative spirit—as it is also a plunge both into the

---

[15] Adrienne Rich, "Transcendental Etude," in *The Dream of a Common Language* (New York: Norton, 1978), xxx.
[16] William Carlos Williams, "Marianne Moore," in *William Carlos Williams: Selected Essays*, 121.
[17] Virginia Woolf, *Mrs Dalloway*. (1925; Oxford: Oxford University Press, 1992), 3.

exigencies of an unknown and into the downward spiral of despair, the depression of "melancholy" as Kenyon describes it, which desires only silence and inertia, desiring death as the only possible extinguishment of its own desiring.

Depressive experiences certainly constitute an important form of "darkness" within Kenyon's poetry, as indeed within her experience,[18] enveloping the speaking voice in melancholic webs of inertia, dissociation and exhaustion, such as in "Rain in January," "When my arm slipped/from the arm of the chair/I let it hang beside me, pale,/useless and strange" (*CP*, 73); or in her most developed work on the topic, "Having It Out with Melancholy":

> A piece of burned meat
> wears my clothes, speaks
> in my voice, dispatches obligations
> haltingly, or not at all.
> It is tired of trying
> to be stouthearted, tired
> beyond measure.
> (*CP*, 233–34)

In Kenyon's poetry, depression is, at least on one level, an earthward drag, an antithetical impulse to the jubilant celebrations of nature which she also recognizes as possible.

When artificially buoyed with medications, the speaker in "Having it Out With Melancholy" can see only the brightness of the day, the life-

---

[18] Kenyon talked openly of her struggle with depressive symptoms, as in the interview with Moyers: "Depression is something I've suffered from all my life. I'm manic-depressive, actually, and I was not properly diagnosed until I was thirty-eight years old. In my case it's more like a unipolar depression … Mine behaves almost like a serious depression only and I rarely become manic …", in *A Hundred White Daffodils*, 153.

affirming possibilities of acceptance, of integration with the natural world:

> High on Nardil and June light
> I wake at four,
> waiting greedily for the first
> notes of the wood thrush. Easeful air
> presses through the screen
> with the wild, complex song
> of the bird, and I am overcome
>
> by ordinary contentment.
> What hurt me so terribly
> all my life until this moment?
> How I love the small, swiftly
> beating heart of the bird
> singing in the great maples;
> its bright, unequivocal eye.
> (CP, 235)

The light here is wonderful—yet it is also excessive, prising open all of the speaker's already heightened senses, in a manner reminiscent of Plath's "Tulips,"[19] where the eye's "stupid pupil" is forced to take in the lively and disturbingly violent colour of the flowers. She is "greedy" for the sound of the bird, alert to the smallest nuance of interior and exterior worlds, emotional and vulnerable in her desire to connect, to love the "small, swiftly/beating heart of the bird." Although linked to her physical experience, as she stands at the screen door at 4am, the dazzling brightness of the summer morning also contrasts with the mystical vision of light she reports earlier in the same poem, when

---

[19] Sylvia Plath. "Tulips," in *Collected Poems*, ed. Ted Hughes (New York: Harper and Row, 1981), 160

> I saw
> that I was a speck of light in the great
> river of light that undulates through time.
>
> I was floating with the whole
> human family. We were all colours – those
> who are living now, those who have died,
> those who are not yet born. For a few
>
> moments I floated, completely calm,
> and I no longer hated having to exist.
> (CP, 232–33)

This light is transcendent, perhaps even somewhat manic, and appears to join the speaker in some kind of spiritual, extra-physical way, with an ultimate *communitas*. It is also a paradox, in that the momentary calm which this river of light brings with it is also in some ways annihilating, something which can be experienced only outside the constraining pathways of ordinary life, outside the house of the physical body. Significantly, the speaker accuses "you"—presumably a personified "melancholy" to whom the poem is addressed—of pulling her out of that "glowing stream," "Like a crow who smells hot blood." It seems an act of mercy—"'I'll hold you up. I never let my dear/ones drown!'"—if the river of light is in fact obliterating, an inexorable tide of desire which leads toward drowning and death. It is also experienced as an act of predation, where melancholy snatches the speaker from her "easeful death" in order to subject her to yet more slow tortures of despair, to "turn me into someone who can't/take the trouble to speak; someone/who can't sleep, or who does nothing/but sleep; can't read, or call/for an appointment for help."

In his interview with Kenyon, Moyers poses the idea that "perhaps depression is itself a gift, a kind of garden in which ideas grow and in which experiences take root."[20] Kenyon agrees insofar as "depression makes me still"—and that stillness is a precondition for the acute paying attention which is necessary for the production of the language and the shape of the poem. This idea that the dark and disturbing shadows of depression can function, in some circumstances, as a fertile ground for creativity, is explored in a number of poems, amongst them "The Beaver Pool in December" (*CP*, 70), and "Depression in Winter" (*CP*, 74). In "The Beaver Pool in December," the poem's speaker sits "in the cold/until dusk," waiting to observe the activity of the beavers as they move into winter. Like many of Kenyon's poems, this poem meticulously evokes a particular landscape, at a particular season, at a particular time of the day, creating an impression of almost documentary reportage:

> The brook is still open
> where the water falls,
> but over the deeper pools
> clear ice forms; over the dark
> shapes of stones, a rotting log,
> and amber leaves that clattered down
> after the first heavy frost.

However, as with so many of Kenyon's poems, it moves also us toward that point of productive confluence, where the interior world of the speaking voice intersects with the specificities of the external world, where the poet's desires are tracked onto and through the precision of the recalled or imagined image of the beavers—industrious, prepared, changing their environment, yet now lost to sight:

> Though I wait in the cold
> until dusk, and though a sudden

---

[20] Bill Moyers, "Interview with Jane Kenyon" (1993), in *A Hundred White Daffodils*, 166.

bubble of air rises under the ice,
I see not a single animal.

The beavers thrive somewhere
else, eating the bark of hoarded
saplings. How they struggled
to pull the long branches
over the stiffening bank …

but now they pass without
effort, all through the chilly
water; moving like thoughts
in an unconflicted mind.

Set again in that liminal zone of dusk, the poet uses the image of the beavers in their freezing pool to create a seemingly idealized picture of a human mind, where what works and labours beneath the surface of consciousness might all be toward a good and rational purpose. Nevertheless, as we follow the position of the speaker—from observer, to imaginer, and back within the implied obscurity of the waters of her own mind—the notion of "conflicted" may not necessarily be construed only as a negative, just as the rational endeavours of a wintering beaver may not constitute the epitome of human aspiration. Indeed the thoughts of a "conflicted mind," although perhaps more difficult to manage on one level, are actually the basis of the poet's creative impulse, the material out of which, as humans, we fashion the complex and imaginative responses to our selves, to our relation to others, as well as to our natural environments. Mental or emotional conflict may be a burden to manage—an almost insupportable burden for some people at some times—but it is also that which feeds the urge to understand and to communicate our understanding to those around us.

In "Depression in Winter," the poem first draws attention to a small space on the south side of a stone on a wintery mountain, the kind of small and specific detail that can be easily missed, not understood:

> There comes a little space between the south
> side of a boulder
> and the snow that fills the woods around it.
> Sun heats the stone, reveals
> a crescent of bare ground; brown ferns,
> and tufts of needles like red hair,
> acorns, a patch of moss, bright green …

Once again, the poem paints a literal image with precision, although the possibilities of the tendrils of metaphoric connection are also immediately signalled with the phrase "There comes …". In the life of the speaker/poet, in the journey of this "I" up the snowy slope, there indeed come points of potential revelation—where the external world is suddenly apparent to the self and where, in that precise clearing of perception, the self can find a space, however small, in which to productively transpose and reflect itself.

> I sank with every step up to my knees,
> throwing myself forward with a violence
> of effort, greedy for unhappiness –
> until by accident I found the stone,
> with its secret porch of heat and light,
> where something small could luxuriate, then
> turned back down my path, chastened and calm.

Paradoxically, the drive that pushes this climber up the mountain with an excessive "violence of effort," seems to derive from a perverse "greed for unhappiness"—a desire for suffering and negativity which may be a destructive end in itself, and/or a way of moving into those very spaces of interior "conflict" which may ultimately yield some form of new insight, a breaking through that would not be found in the easy, apparently smooth path of the frozen surface. Indeed, as "Depression in Winter" unfolds, it is the distilled point where the negative, somewhat reckless flinging forward is arrested—the "accident" of perception—which offers this small window of revelation, the "little space" where snow and cold have not encroached, the "secret porch of heat and light,/where something small could luxuriate." It is not a space or a perception which transforms the entire scene, which remains winter. However, it does offer enough, "a crescent of bare ground" amid desolation, to return the speaker to a more settled path, to bring her back from the bitter heights of extremity to the implied world of the ordinary and blessed world of light and shadow—a blessedness which, paradoxically, would not have been perceivable without the violence, the unhappiness of the climb.

The poem "Peonies at Dusk" (*CP*, 254), finds us again at the uncertain time of twilight,[21] here in Kenyon's garden, where the magnificence of the flowers in the gloaming raises questions about the nature and the source of the light itself:

> White peonies blooming along the porch
> send out light
> while the rest of the yard grows dim.
>
> Outrageous flowers as big as human
> heads! They're staggered
> by their own luxuriance: I had
> to prop them up with stakes and twine.
> The moist air intensifies their scent,
> and the moon moves around the barn

---

[21] See also my discussion of "Things,." "Let Evening Coming," and "Twilight: After Haying" in this context, "Poetry in the Cut: Harvests of Loss and Consolation in the Poetry of Jane Kenyon," *Studio*, vol 1, no. 2 (2007), http://studiojournal.ca/v01n02/studio5b.html

to find out what it's coming from.

In the darkening June evening
I draw a blossom near, and bending close
search it as a woman searches
a loved one's face.

Reminiscent of Pound's haiku-like Imagist fragment, "In a Station of the Metro," [22] the flower is metaphorically equated with the dimensions, beauty and complexity of the human face. Significantly, the blossom is aligned with both the face of the speaker who observes and, from a position of equivalence, "props them up," and also the face of the other, the "loved one" who is caressed and known by the gaze of the poet. The huge white heads of the peonies thus become emblematic of the productive interface between inner and outer, between the self who sees and speaks and the other who is addressed, loved, and who also requires listening to and interpreting. As growing plants, beloved by Kenyon,[23] the peonies also echo the image of the poem as a making, something that may have its own drive and life independent of the poet—yet which is absolutely dependent upon the imagination and artifice of the poet/gardener to bring it into being, to cultivate it to the point of both aesthetic and communicative clarity. The loved other may be equated with the natural magnificence of the flower, but so too is the poem itself. Luminous and fragrant in the falling of night air, the source of its own light, and yet, like the bright, white face of the moon which "moves around the barn/to find out what [the scent] is coming from," the poem, like the peony, is also reflective, communicative, of a light from elsewhere. In this sense the poem, like the peonies, could be seen as its own ordinary miracle; it is

---

[22] Ezra Pound, "In a Station of the Metro": "The apparition of these faces in a crowd;/petals, on a wet, black bough," *Imagist Poetry*, ed. Peter Jones (Harmondsworth: Penguin, 1972), 95.

[23] Cf., for example, Kenyon's essay: "The Moment of Peonies," written for the magazine *Yankee*, and reproduced in *A Hundred White Daffodils*, 46–47.

the beauty of the natural object which is observed, yet it is also the product of that act of observation and intention, orchestrated and propped "with stakes and twine," just as Kenyon carves her personal perceptions into what her husband Donald Hall refers to as the "art of the luminous particular."[24]

Once again, light and dark stand in equivocal symbolic relation to one another. While on the one hand, the almost glowing peonies can be seen as an antidote to the dark, a consoling point of illumination and referentiality in what would otherwise constitute a "dim[ness]," even a fearfulness, it is also the case that the wondrousness of their luminosity, their ability to "send out light" with a presence which amazes even the moon, is in fact accentuated by the falling of the night. The night—be it redolent of darkness, loss, melancholy, death—is thus both a contrast which allows us to read the whiteness of the image or indeed the page, as it is also the condition which facilitates the emotional and linguistic insights of the poem—Moyers' notion of depression as "itself a gift, a kind of garden in which ideas grow and in which experiences take root." As Becky Edgerton notes in her discussion of this poem, Kenyon "confronts agony and faces up to what existence is, but she does so by giving close attention to the concrete."[25]

Reminiscent of Ecclesiastes, Kenyon writes in "Things" (*CP*, 139) of the recognition of the fundamental interchangeability of light and dark, of experience and absence in the cascade of the seasons:

>   Things: simply lasting, then
>   failing to last: water, a blue heron's

---

[24] Donald Hall, "Introduction," in *A Hundred White Daffodils*, x.
[25] Becky Edgerton, "Attention as a Palliative for Depression: The Poems of Jane Kenyon," in *Bright Unequivocal Eye*, 78

> eye, and the light passing
> between them: into light all things
> must fall, glad at last to have fallen.

Only in this interplay of shadow and gleam do we find our place in the world; and only through a paying attention to the particularity of the things of the world—here through the intense looking of the poetic image—do we find comfort and pattern enough to see and accept our inevitable falling, to be "glad at last to have fallen."

Republished from: *Plumwood Mountain* vol. 5 no. 1 Feb. 2014.

Rose Lucas is a Melbourne poet, critic and academic. Her collection of poems, *Even in the Dark,* was published by University of West Australia Press, July 2013. She is currently teaching Poetry and Poetics at Victoria University.

GARRETT HONGO

Hopwood Award: 1975

Did your Hopwood Award impact your approach to subsequent work?

Winning the Hopwood gave me a great boost and validation (as well as paying my way out of town) early on. I'd been in a straight Ph.D. in Japanese literature at the time and I felt there was a conflict between scholarship and my creative interests. Winning the prize gave me more courage to pursue creative interests and, after another summer of intensive language study, I quit the Ph.D. and, although I won in poetry, ran off to Seattle and revived a community theater company dedicated to the production of scripts by Asian American writers. I continued to write poems throughout, of course, and eventually made my way to an MFA at UC Irvine, where I studied with Charles Wright, C.K. Williams, and Howard Moss. And I'm sure letters from Donald Hall and Robert Hayden helped me get in! Finally, it meant something that the judges of the prize I won were Gary Snyder and Ron Padgett and that my manuscript was a lot about the year before I was at Michigan when I lived in a monastery in Kyoto and knocked around the countryside. I felt my voice and perspective were endorsed, that I wasn't so anomalous as a Japanese American poet. The Hopwood award welcomed me into American letters.

Andrea Beauchamp once said that Hopwood winners seem to fall into two groups when they re-read their student manuscripts: pleasantly surprised, or unpleasantly disappointed.

Many poems from my Hopwood manuscript ended up in my first book of poems—*Yellow Light* (Wesleyan, 1982). I still feel good about almost all of them—about a half-dozen or so, I'd guess. Many were crucial—"Issei: First-Generation Japanese American" and "A Restless

Night," both of which are composed as imitations of Chinese poems in translation; "To Mastuo Bashō and Kawai Sora in Nirvana," an address to the great *haiku* poets; and "Postcards for Bert Meyers," a highly imagistic sequence that I wrote for my first teacher, who asked me to describe Kyoto to him. I think poems like these are the foundation of a career-long approach to poetry—image-laden narration that finds a moment poised in lyric arrest, and based on a way of seeing I'd developed from reflecting upon landscape poetry in Chinese and Japanese.

My last question about the formative process in your work has three parts. One, is the obvious and typical question: which poets had the greatest influence on your own approach to writing?

William Wordsworth, Bert Meyers, Charles Wright, and Derek Walcott. I'd discovered Wordsworth as a sophomore in a Romantic Poets class and what M.H. Abrams calls his *greater romantic lyrics* just stuck with me as both emotional and structural models. Later, at a crisis point in my poetry, I wrote a book-length "prose" work called *Volcano: A Memoir of Hawai'i* that's in a very strong sense modeled after *The Prelude* in terms of chronicling the growth of a poetic inspiration—a native landscape I'd been born to but that I was made absent from since infancy and later returned to as an adult. The immensity of the project of describing the volcano, rain forest, and family history daunted me, asked more of me than I could accomplish in my current poetic style, so I devised a language and a book that could swallow that larger imagistic and informational feast, a book that wasn't actually prose, but a form of English I styled after the *haibun* of Bashō, the *zuihitsu* of Yoshida Kenkō, and the prose of Herman Melville from the *Cetology* chapters of *Moby-Dick*. When I first met with my editor, Sonny Mehta of Knopf, in revising the first draft of the book, he turned to me, reading glasses perched on his nose, and said, "Garrett, *now* I understand why it took you so long to write this book! It's not *prose*, is it?" It was not.

Two, did any so-called "schools" of poetry impress you or influence your work?

I'd say the imagistic tradition in English was highly influential—Pound's translations from the Chinese in *Cathay* (along with *The Seafarer*), Rexroth and Snyder's translations from the Chinese (and their own poetry), and then, finally, Bert Meyers and Charles Wright, both magnificent imagistic poets who also developed their own refined, ornate (to the point of being even opaque at times) poetic diction to accompany it.
Beyond the imagistic, I've pursued poets of rhetorical finish and complexity—Anthony Hecht, Derek Walcott, and Charles Wright—and gone back and studied Sidney, Keats, Yeats, Hopkins, Pound, *et al* in a similar pursuit.

But I've not at all gone after the kinds of schools tagged with a catchy name of any kind. Not the Beats, not the Confessionals or Objectivists, not the poets of Deep Image nor of Projective Verse. I've tended to cherry-pick, mostly.

Third (and last), are you aware of (or care to share) any non-literary influences that have been especially important to your writing: music, visual art, social change, environmentalism, etc.?

Oh, yes! American post-bop and "cool" jazz — the improvisatory principles, the suppleness and intertwining of rhythms, the heteroglossia. I listened to Miles Davis's *Kind of Blue* all the time in trying to write my first poems as an undergraduate at Pomona College, probably wrote a two of the poems I'd already mentioned as being from my Hopwood manuscript. And John Coltrane's *Ballads* and Charles Mingus's *Oh Yeah* and *Mingus Ah Um*. And German chamber music—Beethoven's String Quartet No. 7, the "Razumovsky," as played by the Budapest String Quartet. The Mendelssohn Octet and Brahms Sextet in B flat major too, as performed by Heifetz and Piatigorsky with Primrose, *et al.* That richness of string sound and complicated and overlapping syntactic lines like a rhetoric. Those were the LPs in heavy circulation as I begun to try to write poetry as a sophomore and junior in college. It's the soundtrack to my poetic upbringing.

In narrative, I think Japanese balladry in *enka* and *min'yo* became significant the more I learned about them. It's a style of compressed storytelling with a powerful tragic or melancholic edge that I think my narrative poems have internalized. I'd heard them as a child growing up in Hawaiʻi and recognized them like lost childhood playmates when I studied them in a course in Japanese music while in graduate school at Michigan. Appalachian ballads, Scots-Irish ballads, and a lot of American country & western songs are close kin to these, as, of course, are the lyrical ballads of Coleridge and Wordsworth.

Finally, liberation and ethnic studies movements were important too—black liberation, black literature of the 60s and early 70s, the socio-cultural defiant stances of Quincy Troupe and Stanley Crouch as African American poets, the emergence of Asian American Studies at UCLA and Long Beach State, and the kind, multi-cultural tutelage of Robert Hayden at Michigan were all significant.

A question perhaps particularly pertinent to you, Garrett Hongo, emerges from your 2012 interview with Lantern Review Blog. To quote: "I wanted to see if I could create a prose that was like poetry…….. It indeed was about the growth of my own poetic mind, to see if I could, like a python, dislocate my poetic jaws and swallow a huge and gorgeous landscape, all those ostensibly non-poetic subjects like geology, volcanology, rain forest biology, oral family histories, and local talk story. I'd felt my own poetry too confined to take on that Volcano world, so I turned to prose, but not a prose of reportage or standard non-fiction. It had to have the weight of meditation, aimed for the capture of fleeting insights and inspiration like poetry."

My follow-up question would be, would you care to share any perceptions of whether and how that experience of creating a prose that was like poetry may have impacted your subsequent work as a poet, writing within the genre we call "poetry?"

I've addressed some of this in a response to another question, but, specifically, I think having written *Volcano* influenced me to adopt a much longer but still imagistically freighted line from then on. If you look at *Coral Road* and the poems appearing in magazines now, you'll see a broad-shouldered poetic line much longer than the normative lines in the earlier books (with some notable exceptions—"The Unreal Dwelling: My Years in Volcano," the dramatic monologue in my paternal grandfather's voice from *The River of Heaven*, being most significant). My poems since *Volcano* might also be more open to discursive asides or digressions than before, incorporate more information and anecdotes, and allow for more tonal shifts. I remember C.K. Williams, one of my other teachers, saying, while he was writing *With Ignorance* and *Tar*, that he'd broken with his earlier, more compressed lyric work and that he wanted a poem that could be open to *anything*—philosophy, sociology, reflection, and story—as well as carry a potent lyric and political punch. I don't think I've accomplished that myself, but I'm now certainly much more open to more varieties of poetic expression than my earlier lyric and narrative poems allowed me to incorporate.

In terms of sharing poetry beyond printed books and journals, have you found poetry readings to be useful or enjoyable? Have you been at all attracted to, or intrigued by, the option of sharing poetry (or musings about poetry) online via social media or similar digital venues?

I like giving readings, though I'm no longer that enamored of myself at the podium. I used to make a big part of my living giving readings around the country but that also took me away from my sons in their early childhood and we never got that back. Then, the University of

Oregon got me a nice raise several years ago so I wouldn't have to chase income elsewhere so much, and I got to stay home more and my youngest child, my daughter, had the benefit of that and so did I. That said, I enjoy sharing the work, telling stories, and meeting new people at the readings I do give nowadays. I'm giving several book store, art gallery, and community cultural center readings this year and happy to do them. And I was happy touring *Coral Road* when it came out in 2011, reading at universities, colleges, and cultural centers around the country.

I've read for digital venues when asked, either single poems being published online with audio clips attached, or podcasts I think they're called. But I haven't generated such myself. Recently, the University of Arizona Poetry Center put online a lecture I gave on the Justice Department Detention Centers during WW II—different than the internment camps in that these housed exclusively men (community leaders, intelligentsia, and those suspected of fifth column activity)—and that history as background to my sequence of poems that are the fictive letters of Kubota, my maternal grandfather. I thought I spoke pretty well—succinctly, informatively—in a casual manner about a terrible time in America and my own family history. I was glad they did that.

Do you see modern academia in general as a good professional base for working poets? Do you feel the role of the poet in the academy has had any discernible impact—positive or negative—upon poetry in general in the U.S. and/or the U.K.?

It's been a great boon to the production of poetry and the opening of it as a literary genre to diversity of social groups and classes than before these kinds of university appointments had become regular and normal. And I've enjoyed career-long support from universities myself—the paycheck, benefits, and retirement contributions and all.

But, at the same time, it's been wearing to have to attend to the constant and increasingly demanding bureaucratic choring and bullshit monetization of our time and teaching. The contemporary university has abandoned the liberal arts imperatives of creating thoughtful, literate, and informed individuals in favor of ideas of students as "units" and their instruction as "outcomes" and "measurables." I find these latest trends to be of the manufacture from "the Satanic mills," as William Blake called them, and they undermine the humanistic calling and mission I'd thought I'd entered when choosing the profession of university professor.

Here, I'd like to offer you the option of posing a question to yourself that perhaps you've never been asked, or wish you had been asked. Or, perhaps, revisit a question from some past interview that you would now answer differently, or from a changed perspective.

What can be the artistic function and consequences of such a prize as the Hopwood, in your estimation?

It does a lot of things. It creates an immediate monetary and social validation for one's interest and gifts in literary writing first of all. But, over time, I think it also creates a loose fellowship of associations—a cast of predecessors and luminaries, even fellows, that can provide a kind of imaginary company of support as well. It mattered to me that Arthur Miller and Frank O'Hara had once won it, but it mattered even more that writers I'd get to know later, after I left Michigan —Al Young, Ted Solotaroff, Cid Corman, Robert Hayden, Howard Moss (later a teacher), and Leonard Michaels had won it as well—and having won it was part of their welcome of me, I'd say. And I still can remember Robert Hayden walking up to me in the Hopwood Room and shaking my hand in congratulations one afternoon. It was like a gentle bolt of lightning. All of it mattered to me in the days of obscurity I was to endure as I tried to create myself as a poet during the late 70s and establish a career at it thereafter. Finally, things have gone full-circle recently, as I served as a judge of the prizes a few years ago and thought long and hard about what it might mean as a recognition and validation for the young poet I happened to be reading in the contest. I wanted to encourage as much as evaluate, recognize promise as much as accomplishment, and divine what was earnest and deep in the work that I thought might have the best chance to persist over a lifespan. It was a cool thing to have done and I'm grateful to have had opportunities both as a winner and as a judge.

DONALD BEAGLE

Hopwood Award: 1977

[Interviewed by Barbara Tierney, Head, Research and Information Services, University Libraries; University of Central Florida. UCF's burgeoning enrollment of 60,000+ now includes students in one of the newer MFA Creative Writing programs in the U.S., chaired by poet Terry Ann Thaxton, MFA.]

Did your Hopwood award impact your approach to subsequent work?

Winning the Hopwood Award in the "major poetry" category was a welcome validation, along with the very encouraging commentary by judge Lawrence Lieberman, and the A+ I'd received from Radcliffe Squires for my independent study. In a sense, the award started an early streak of good fortune: my poems soon began appearing in journals like *Carolina Quarterly*, followed by my successful stint teaching evening poetry workshops at Duke University (my day job —as it remains today —was as a library director, then in a public library system near Chapel Hill NC, now for 20 years as a tenured professor at Belmont Abbey College in Charlotte NC).

But this early run of good fortune was suddenly interrupted when, giving a routine speech one day in the 1980's, my voice simply quit working. I rushed to Duke Medical Center where they diagnosed me with "adult onset dysphonia." Dysphonia is a neuromuscular disorder that tends to strike in the mid-30's. While it usually plateaus leaving some residual voice behind, the normal voice rarely recovers. My normal voice has never recovered, and there is *still* no cure 30+ years later. It has nothing to do with stage fright. My vocal chords malfunction just as acutely reading a bedtime story to our granddaughter as when I am attempting to give a conference presentation, or trying to read a poem aloud in a bookstore. Perhaps the most well-known dysphonia sufferer, reporter Dianne Rheem of National Public Radio, has found some relief from Botox injections into her vocal tract. I tried that treatment in the late 1990's but found no improvement.

While this disorder did not greatly impair my library career (library directors can whisper without terrible consequences), it diminished the pleasure I'd felt giving poetry readings, and undermined normal audience feedback (typical reaction: "Oh, you sound terrible, poor thing. You must have horrible allergies.") More importantly, I felt I had to abandon leading the Duke University workshops, which had been an even more valuable source of personal creative growth. I did work the dysphonia experience (with its unrelenting and oft-exhausting struggle to make myself heard and understood) into a few poems, such as the beginning of "Sullivan's Island:"

> This is the land of lost years left in shells.
> Each day I walk to the ocean to say nothing;
> My mouth is the shell of something that swam away.

But its biggest impact was in my hoped-for transition from Hopwood manuscript to debut published collection. For years after my natural voice vanished, every time a press editor would express interest in publishing my 1st collection, the deal would crash and burn on the news that I could not help promote my book on any reading circuit. That never stopped my writing, but did gradually turn me into a desk-drawer-hoarder poet for decades. The original rhythmic, incantatory voice I had hoped to externalize and project to the larger world turned inward; becoming instead a sort of subliminal echo of a partially hidden self. I am not trolling for sympathy; but it would be absurd, indeed dishonest, to not mention the dysphonia, or to pretend it had no impact. Over those years I declined to resort to a vanity press, or to use Amazon self-publishing. Fortunately, my morale was sustained a bit by a few awards after the Hopwood that required no public readings— the John Brubaker Award in 2011, two prize winning poems in the annual Ekphrasis Contest (2013 and 2017), and others. But it was finally the innovation of a new type of peer-reviewed scholarly press independently based in large academic libraries, like Stanford University Library's HighWire Press and Wake Forest University's Library Partners Press, that established this new model for a non-profit academic publisher with no need for a poet to do promotional readings.

When X. J. Kennedy offered his wonderful review comments in January 2017 about my oft-delayed but newly-published collection *What Must Arise: Poems,* he quickly noted that I was then 63, and added the side-note in his follow-up letter: "Possibly the most long-overdue debut collection in recent history!" Another reviewer who knew my personal history perceptively commented that I now face an interesting dilemma in subsequent books: how to balance my new work against the urge to pull old poems out of that accumulated 40-year hoard to finally see them in print collections. Very true—this is quickly becoming an interesting balancing act, because I don't want to rest on that hoard. I intend to do everything I can to keep growing as a writer into my mid-60's and hopefully beyond. In fact, I quite deliberately left *What Must Arise* a good deal shorter than it could easily have become, because I didn't want it to be an exercise in excavation. My new collection-in-progress, *Driving Into the Dreamtime,* has some twenty-four new poems (thus far) and five salvaged from the archives through multiple revisions.

Andrea Beauchamp once said that Hopwood winners seem to fall into two groups when they re-read their student manuscripts: pleasantly surprised, or unpleasantly disappointed.

I am definitely in this latter group. I sympathize with John Ciardi's half-humorous threat to break into the Hopwood Room some night to abscond with his winning manuscript. But some things from that student assemblage have resurfaced over the years. The poem "On Whitefish Bay" floated into my first collection with relatively minor revisions. Other bits and pieces of Hopwood-period poems re-emerged in differing guises or disguises. I no longer have a copy of that full student manuscript, but I believe it included an early poem titled "Elegy After Rilke." A few of the better lines from that poem returned to memory when I read new work by San Francisco poet Tamsin Smith in her book, *Word Cave*. Four of her phrases triggered such resonances, resulting in my sequence "Four Fantasias on Lines by Tamsin Smith."

Which poets have influenced your own approach to writing poetry—ranging from "classics" to any contemporaries who may have influenced your mature work? Also, did any so-called "schools" of poetry impress you?

I should mention my first encounter with a famous author, who happened to not be a poet. Around 1967, Cranbrook Academy (north of Detroit) started a summer arts immersion program for high school students called "Adventure in Creativity." By 1969 it had grown too big for Cranbrook's facilities, so they partnered with nearby Oakland University (Rochester MI). My parents somehow scraped together the $800 to let me attend in the summer of 1970. When I walked into the first session of the creative writing class, the first fellow-student I met introduced herself as Anne Serling. Fast forward to the end of summer when I had the chance to briefly meet her father, screenwriter Rod Serling. Serling's comments about how much he liked my student poems in the Adventure's summer writing magazine gave me a crucial boost of inspirational motivation. Anne and I still correspond, by the way, after these many years, and we still exchange draft writings and commentaries. Her own wonderful 2014 memoir, *As I Knew Him*, captures her father's unique genius with great insight and eloquence. Serling's storytelling genius, to me, entailed a powerful narrative energy that also incorporated probing (and sometimes biting) social commentary. My poem "Television" is dedicated "To Anne Serling and her father, Rod."

The Michigan countryside of rural East Liberty, about 45 miles west of Ann Arbor, had already grounded me in the romantics, post-romantics, and neo-romantics, spanning Europeans from Keats to Yeats, and Americans ranging from Whitman to Dickinson, along with my longstanding personal fetish for Poe. In due time, the fine English Department faculty at Oakland University ushered me into the 20th century, from Dylan Thomas to Sylvia Plath and beyond. My undergraduate EN Honors Thesis on allusions to *Dracula* in Eliot's "The Waste Land" became my first academic publication, and is still being cited 40 years later.

Then, after spending a year away from college to stand in as adjunct-instructor for Harriet Stolorow's Poetry Workshop at JCC (while she took sabbatical to begin her dissertation), I finally found my way to graduate school in Ann Arbor. The one UM faculty poet whose work most impacted my own would have to be Radcliffe Squires. I won't focus on Squires here because this Q&A will be followed later in this book by a second interview done with me by Charleston poet Frances Pearce, about my motivation to assemble, edit, and introduce the 2017 book, *Radcliffe Squires: Selected Poems 1950-1985*. But it was Squires who helped me learn how to let each poem find its own unique denouement without being ensnared in academic "isms." Perhaps most importantly over the long haul, I learned from Radcliffe how to overcome my impatience with the vital and inevitable processes of continual reassessment and revision. Accordingly, I can say that more than half of the poems from *What Must Arise* will have at least minor revisions when they reappear in my forthcoming *Driving Into the Dreamtime: New & Selected Poems*.

Regarding "schools" of poetry, I was certainly cognizant in the late 1970's of the Imagists, the Confessionals, the Beats, the Black Mountain poets, and so forth. But I also think my poetry was strengthened by my decisions at multiple points to not pursue literary studies in isolation. Even as an undergraduate freshman, before my transfer to Oakland University, I had first entered the California Institute of the Arts —then a hotbed of avant-garde pedagogy —with a rare double-major in music (piano) and creative writing. My CalArts prose course with novelist Mark Harris (*Bang the Drum Slowly*, etc.) acquainted me with his psycholinguist wife, Josephine, who recruited me into her own remarkable trimester writing seminar, "Monologue-Dialogue-Discourse." CalArts later temporarily shuttered its Creative Writing / Critical Studies program, so over summer 1973 I transferred back to Oakland University in Michigan, to start my sophomore year. Following Josephine's advice, I supplemented my BA in English Literature with a Concentration in Linguistics. This included a trip to the Summer Linguistics Institute at UMass/Amherst in 1974. There, I plunged into an immersive study of the remarkable book co-authored by Noam Chomsky and his MIT colleague, Morris Halle: *The Sound Pattern of English*. Chomsky is best known, of course, for his works on transformational (or generative) grammar, such as *Syntactic Structures*. But *The Sound Pattern of English* is an equally groundbreaking analytical study of English phonology. Its findings then propelled Halle to work with Samuel Jay Keyser of UMass / Amherst on the development of a new theory of metrics in poetry that came to be known as the Halle-Keyser Theory.

My metrical theory course that summer in Amherst was personally team-taught by Halle and Keyser, highlighted by a lengthy Institute-wide lecture by Noam Chomsky. I have never (to my knowledge) met another poet who studied Chomsky's *The Sound Pattern of English* in similar depth, and very few who have even read the Halle-Keyser follow-up book, *English Stress: Its Form, Its Growth and Its Role in Verse*. I gained much more by absorbing that content directly and personally from those remarkable linguists than I would have by simply reading their research from afar. The insights I learned that summer still figure in my ongoing efforts to explore new variants of quasi-metrical patterning in my own poems, without becoming what would typically be termed a "new formalist." (Or does my research into phonology actually make me a "new formalist" in some divergent way?).

Perhaps I was receptive to this research because my rural East Liberty childhood had included attending one of the last one-room schools in Michigan, with 35 fellow-students, grades one through six. (Hopwood poet Jane Kenyon, by the way, also attended a Michigan one-room school). In that era, the one-room elementary school assured I had already absorbed a pedagogy of reading based on "phonics." This entailed concepts such as "sharp and flat" (and "long and short") vowel-sounds. Note the musical parallel with sharp and flat notes, which to me, as a young "prodigy" pianist, implied that patterns of sharp and flat vowel sequences could possibly (if subtly) emulate melodic phrase-structures. (Linguists do not now properly describe vowels as sharp or flat, of course, using the more precise terminology of "tense" and "lax.") I use "sharp" and "flat" here merely as a descriptive vernacular shorthand. One brief example would be the following excerpt from my poem "After the Bruckner Eighth:"…wandering past ranks and rows of trees / withered militia under winter's fire / with massive batteries of Manhattan's grayglass towers as glacial backdrop / aspiring to the sky…" The first two lines are a series of flat vowel-sequences (wandering / past / ranks) and (withered / militia / winter), enjambed into line-ending sharps (trees), (fire). The third line concludes this part of the poem's phrase-structure by beginning with flats (massive / batteries / Manhattan), followed by double trochaic sharp-flats (grayglass), (glacial), finally culminating in a flat-sharp-flat-flat-sharp sequence (aspiring to the sky).

Each of my poems plays with such vowel-clusters and consonant sequences in its own unique way, depending on that poem's structural syllabics. A more complex example from my book would be "New Years Eve in a Manhattan Penthouse," where the poem's sound patterns (influenced by Chomsky-Halle-Keyser), reinforces its social commentary (inspired by Serling). Here, I try to use sharp vowel-clusters, which tend to impart tension (slide / widely / aside / guide / sky), to tighten the initial sense of that toxic predatory environment of Wall Street. These are followed by flat vowel clusters reinforcing a sense of disturbing or unsettling consequences played out over a lengthy "v" consonant sequencing (nervous / envious / covetous / rival / vast / canvas / invented / veranda / overseers / overlook / rivers / investments). Consonant sequences *within* words (internal alliteration, so to speak) can create a tonal counterpoint that functions almost like a *continuo* line in chamber music. I am, of course, neglecting here the vital role of imagery and metaphor, which are equally important in my work. But these would take too much space to describe.

To shift focus a moment, I think Charles Olson's "projective verse" essay, drawing on his Black Mountain College experience, about underlying relationships between the rhythms of breath and the poetic line, might well have attained more interesting and persuasive dimensions had Olson been able to develop his concepts in light of the later phonological discoveries by Chomsky, Halle, and Keyser. This perspective can also inform the ongoing studies of the so-called "Poet Voice," as discussed in the article: "Beyond Poet Voice: Sampling the (Non-) Performance Styles of 100 American Poets," by MacArthur, Zellou, and Miller, in *Cultural Analytics* April 18, 2018. Poet Lisa Marie Basile has called this "Poet Voice" phenomenon a "flock mentality;" I think the Chomsky-Halle approach would perhaps equate "Poet Voice" with something akin to a "peer-group prestige dialect." If such peer-group psychology weighs this heavily on many modern poets, I suspect it weighs even more heavily on poetry anthologists, contest judges, and editors of literary journals.

Now that your first collection has finally been published, have you gained any new insights at age 63 from reviews or reader reactions to the poems it contains?

Thankfully, response has been overwhelmingly favorable, even as frequent readers of contemporary poetry have noted that my work is distinctive, and not necessarily in the stylistic or substantive mainstream of typical fare in the journals, or in the frontlists of publishers like Copper Canyon or Graywolf. That's fine by me. I've even been called an "outlier" –a label I've always relished and celebrated. From Day One in Ann Arbor I rigorously avoided the typical English MA or MFA track in favor of Library / Information Science because my overriding goal is to pursue my personal voice and vision wherever they might lead. I've never wanted my creative energies to be influenced by any academic quota of poems-published-per-year. Perhaps this helps explain why three distinctive groupings of favorite poems seem to have emerged from among my book's readership. Those readers (and fellow poets) who seem to read contemporary journals most frequently, have been the ones most likely to favor poems like "The Jellyfish," "The Lost Sister," "The Shroud," and "The Night Watchman." But another distinctive group has emerged, exemplified by a nationally-known scientist and a widely-published folklore scholar, both of whom peruse poetry collections as a fairly intense but only occasional side-interest. This group of highly-educated readers, who are less exposed to the editorial norms and stylistic presuppositions of the journals, seems to coalesce around a set of favorite poems that typically includes "Home Movie," "The Genealogists," "Television," and "Touring a Nuclear Reactor." In fact, the folklore scholar (whom I've never met) somehow found my college library office number and phoned me from her condo in Manhattan. She then literally recited aloud to me the complete text of "Touring a Nuclear Reactor." I was floored, because she had been trained in professional acting, so hearing that poem recited with her oratorical expertise felt revelatory. (Needless to say, she did not use "Poet Voice!") As with the "Manhattan Penthouse" poem, the sound pattern of the "Nuclear Reactor" poem (which I won't explicate here because its phrase-structure complexity would require pages of explanation) overlays a deeper level of Serling-esque social commentary.

Touring a Nuclear Reactor

The guide leads his line of dutiful tourists
past gray-suited guards, into a corridor
where shoes click on tile and the echoes
ricochet like ticks in a Geiger counter.

We intuit an inner chamber, but detour
into a classroom with dayglow chairs
where we are lectured that nuclear reactors
are bought with bonds, like schools and wars.

Now we must empty our pockets and pass
like mendicants between magnetic detectors
lest one of us (a terrorist) unexpectedly explodes.
We enter the chamber: cool as a hospital, tall

as a cathedral. We stand on a stainless-steel
mezzanine, the pool of perfect water below
from where blue floodlights glow like the sky
of Nepal. We know, in that liquid-crystal abyss

of a dark place, cloistered and devious,
where matter was pitted against itself, where a bit
of the world, contradicted, disappeared, and in its
place appeared the perjurious heart of fire.

It is time, we are told, to depart, and so we pass
from the peristyle like a whispering choir
to see in the exit hall one final display:

the Atomic Clock. Ticking with a lunatic

precision, it re-echoes the echoing particles
of itself. The guide clicks his hand-counter
as each of us obediently leaves, while the cooling
tower traces its hourglass over the trees.

The scientist emailed me with his own perspective: *"I suspect that if poems from our time are still being read a century from now, readers will likely be interested in how our poets and novelists interpreted this tidal wave of new technologies currently sweeping over our culture. I'm betting your poems like "Television," "Home Movie," "The Genealogists," and "Touring a Nuclear Reactor" have a real chance to be among the poems those descendants of ours will still be reading and discussing. I say that because, to me, these poems explore our interactions with those technologies on both perceptual and metaphysical levels."* All I could say in reply was "You, sir, are the sort of reader every poet must dream about." What I did not say to him, but I will say here, is that I especially value the responses of readers like the scientist and the folklore scholar because, to me, they exemplify that wider potential audience for poetry that many modern American journal editors, book publishers, and anthologists have sadly "lost."

Lastly, I've heard from quite a few readers who, like Michael Joyce, Professor of Creative Writing and Media Studies at Vassar, seem to especially like the musical poems: "On Attending the World Premier of Hydrogen Jukebox," "After the Bruckner Eighth," and "On Performing Bach's Dorian Toccata." My motivation to do poems about those three composers (Glass, Bruckner, and Bach) certainly reflects how their music became neglected and / or misperceived by audiences and critics for extended periods—again, through that odd and largely unexamined intersection between peer-group psychology and conventional wisdom. Of course, these poems also grew from a deeply personal motivation; I had grown up as a bit of a musical prodigy, playing our Yamaha grand piano from age six. My successful audition for the CalArts School of Music had included Bach's Dorian Toccata; the Prelude & Fugue #2 from Bach's Well-Tempered Clavier, two etudes by Chopin, and Beethoven's *Pathétique* Sonata. Music has always remained an essential (if slightly quarrelsome) life-partner with my motivation to write poetry. And a few stylistic features that mark me as an outlier do remind me just a bit of some early critiques directed at Philip Glass' intentional use of highly repetitive rhythmic motifs embedded within surprisingly traditional harmonics.

Drawing on Chomsky-Halle *Sound Pattern* concepts, I play with those alternating sharp vs. flat patterns within a more plain-spoken rhetorical style to underscore a poem's semantics. One of the clearest examples can be found in "The Genealogists," which explores how modern technology weirdly intermeshes our subjective perceptions of past, present, and future. The poem plays with this concept using sometimes parallel, sometimes alternating, sounds and imagery, in sync with its patterning of sharp, median, and flat sequences of vowel-clusters.

> The Genealogists
>
> To find them, you must enter the library at night
> and descend the dark stair that at first appears
> to lead nowhere, but leaves you, at length, face
> to face with a door. Open this door with care.
> You will not want to disturb them, sitting in dim
> rows, their eyes bluegreen from their microfilm
> dream. And you, with your scandalous
> ancestors and creaking shoes, are the intruder here.
> But if you are humble they will tolerate your descent
> and permit you to peer over their shoulders
> upon the austere screens. You may wonder
> what and who they are searching for, hunched over
> as if in prayer, in hushed postures before their
> purring machines. You clearly wish to inquire

> of the frail-looking woman in the rear
> whose frosted hair glimmers like an elegiac star.
> She will smile at you, and whisper, in a voice
> age has chided to cracked ice, her Byzantine lies.
> These are the genealogists, and cannot tell us
> why they are here, staring at ship manifests,
> court minutes, simulacra of the dearly departed,
> on reels unwinding like atoms of antimatter.
> Do not touch her, therefore, or you will both disappear
> with a vanishing flash, into that void where the future
> revisits us, the negative of an invisible past.

To conclude, in a time when editors seem to seize upon poems that unfold as imagistic word-streams with constant novelty, unpredictability, and relentlessly oblique angles of expression and insight, my more normative, sometimes repetitive style probably feels to them like the expressive "flatness" some early critics ascribed to the music of Philip Glass. Regardless, my writing style is always directed toward maximizing each poem's holistic expressive presence, rather than toward seeing how deftly or adroitly it can attenuate the reader's expectations at every possible juncture. But let me also say that I very much enjoy and admire those poets whose work does undermine lazy preconceptions of normative form—some poets of that description are in this book.

Have you ever regretted pursuing Library / Information Science as a "9-5" profession?

No, but my answer entails an unexpected irony, because in 1976-77 I expected this career choice to provide the sort of stable yet mundane livelihood that Wallace Stevens presumably found in insurance. But through no master plan of my own, fate and circumstance allowed my academic writings to have a significant and provably global impact. When the Internet / World Wide Web exploded circa 1995, many of us directing libraries suddenly realized we were at one of the great pivot-points of history, equal to Gutenberg's printing press: the initial fault line between the Age of Print and the Digital Age. Academic libraries first tried to cope by installing generic computer labs in traditional reference departments. That didn't work, for too many reasons to explain here. A handful of university libraries then tried a new experimental model, first called the Information Commons, and later, the Learning Commons. I was hired by UNC-Charlotte to start an Information Commons in 1997. At the time it was only the 6th or 7th in the U.S., and I began publishing a series of articles that drew wide attention, culminating in in 2010, when I was invited to author the lead article for the 50th anniversary issue of the *Journal of Library Administration*—a special issue devoted to the Information Commons.[26] Even earlier, my first book, *The Information Commons Handbook* (ALA / Neal-Schuman, 2006) was published, and has become the most-cited book on the topic. Now there are many hundreds of these Learning Commons; probably between 500 and 600 across the U.S. and Canada, with hundreds more in Europe and across the Pacific Rim. Lest anyone doubt the global impact, the Japanese translation of my later article ("The Learning Commons in Historical Context") can be found in the Nagoya University Cloud Repository. And Purdue University Press has archived the interview (and photo) done with me following my 2005 invited lecture at Deutscher Bibliothekartag in Düsseldorf.[27]

Architect Alex Couchman emailed me from Auckland to say "You probably have no idea how many people in Australia and New Zealand are reading your book," and French architect Catherine Closét-Crane

---

[26] Beagle, Donald. (2010) 'The Emergent Information Commons: Philosophy, Models, and 21st Century Learning Paradigms', *Journal of Library Administration*, 50: 1, 7 — 26. Available at:< http://dx.doi.org/10.1080/01930820903422347 >

[27] Tierney, Barbara (2007) "ATG Interviews Donald Beagle," *Against the Grain*: Vol. 19: Iss. 3, Article 15. Available at: <
https://docs.lib.purdue.edu/cgi/viewcontent.cgi?article=5372 >

emailed me from Paris to let me know she was basing much of her Ph.D. dissertation on my research (Catherine's work was later published in English under the title: *A Critical Analysis of the Discourse on Academic Libraries as Learning Places*.) It still fascinates me to visit these facilities, ranging from the Brody Learning Commons at Johns Hopkins University to the Rolex Learning Center at École Polytechnique in Lausanne, Switzerland, and learn how my writings influenced the built environment. It is remarkable to watch university students crowding into a new $25 million building, and have a tour guide introduce me as "The father of the Information Commons." (A label I always discourage, by the way). So, yes, it has been fascinating to see my writings have such an unusually tangible impact. I certainly never planned for this, just as I never expected my research to be featured in the article on "Academic Libraries" in the *Encyclopedia of Information Science & Technology*. (IGI Global, 2014; 3rd edition). But I will point out one interesting "common" thread underlying this that is inextricably linked to my approach to poetry: the radical pedagogy practiced in the single labyrinthine building of the California Institute of the Arts I had sought out in the early 1970's drew upon the experimental pedagogy of the 1930's "Studies Building" at Black Mountain College, which in turn attempted to re-instantiate the uniquely focused ambiance of those archaic one-room schools like the one-room elementary school I attended in rural Michigan. All of those examples flowed inexorably toward the underlying concepts we now see articulated in the modern Learning Commons. This developmental process points toward a future where poets, composers, filmmakers, and creative artists in all media and genres can collaborate in innovative learning spaces using leading-edge technologies.

LAURA KASISCHKE

Hopwood Awards: 1981; 1982; 1983; 1984

[**Editor's Note**: My original intent had been to do yet another Q&A conversation with Laura Kasischke. But when I viewed the "Poets at Michigan" video series, I was struck by how Laura's superb poetry reading in video #3 ("The Art Continues"), included comments about her student and faculty experiences at the University of Michigan, along with reflections on the early origins and development of her own poetry. These commentaries were vividly brought to life by the vibrant immediacy of the poems themselves. Because both her comments and her poems reflected the context of her life during her collegiate and faculty career, they offered insightful perspectives on the poet's formative campus experiences as well as her own inimitable creative process. I thank both LSA and Laura Kasischke for permission to publish this excerpted transcript.][28]

"It is impossible to name all the fantastic poets who have been associated with this place, but I don't think I've heard anyone [*at this reading*] say the name Frank O'Hara. So I just want to say I want to read a poem, this poem by Frank O'Hara. He has a wonderful poem, "Ann Arbor Variations," which is one of my favorites, but a little long, too long to read. This is just a short one and I think of him sitting on the steps of Angell Hall writing this poem:

---

[28] "Poets at Michigan, Then and Now— The Art Continues: Contemporary Michigan Poets." Featuring Jamaal May, Airea D. Matthews, and Laura Kasischke. University of Michigan College of Literature, Science, and the Arts. (May 1, 2017). Available at: https://www.youtube.com/watch?v=OyjIq1D-IP4&t=1551s

Animals

Have you forgotten what we were like then
When we were still first rate
And the day came with an apple in its mouth

It's no use worrying about Time
But we did have a few tricks up our sleeves
and turned some sharp corners

the whole pasture looked like our meal
we didn't need speedometers
we could manage cocktails out of ice and water

I wouldn't want to be faster
or greener than now if you were with me O you
were the best of all my days

…I was at another university this weekend. I hadn't looked very carefully at my itinerary and suddenly saw that I would be ushered into a room where there was going to be an hour and a half of Q&A. and I thought *an hour and a half of Q&A*?! [*laughter*] So I immediately started calling up, getting calls up on my iPhone and I thought would kill some time talking about Roethke and Robert Frost and reading them, or something, Then I realized that as a special punishment for their undergrads, they made everybody come to the Q&A, and made every student ask a question, and there were like two hundred were there! [*laughter*] But as I was going up with my phone, my host said 'don't worry, we won't let them read their questions off their iPhones.' Oh, yeah; that would be so tacky! [*laughter*]…

…I was in a retrospective mood thinking about reading at this event. I have had pretty much every role at the University of Michigan that you can have. I don't know what else it would be. I was a student here, so I have had the blessing of great teachers and classmates and roommates and even had a couple evil roommates, but not evil teachers [*laughter*]…then some of those teachers have gone on to be my colleagues, and I've had wonderful colleagues. And then I am a Michigan Mom; my son is a junior here; and then the crowning glory of it all is having students here. When I die, they'll have to mix my ashes with the cement and put it in a parking structure [*laughter*]. So then I will have been and done everything.

…Anyway I hauled out this poem that I'm pretty sure I wrote when I was an undergraduate here. Either that or I got the idea for it by cutting out a newspaper article. And I still have that and have the date on that I wrote the poem in response to this headline about something which happened in Indiana: "Woman kills sweetheart with bowling ball." Whoever wrote that headline, there were a lot of other ways to express that, like "Man brutally murdered by girlfriend." [*laughter*] But no, the title is:

Woman Kills Sweetheart with Bowling Ball

The moon is loose in the gutter tonight
and it rolls without kisses
or handprints between us Its mouth
Is an O of surprise

O Tonight the phantasma of love
climbs the stairs while we sleep She
sags with exhaustion and booze
and pills while her skin hangs heavy
and empty as hate
She floats so slow she floats
as if she were swimming through blood

Shhh Shhh the lights are out
and the little suspicion
sleeps and dreams
and whimpers in its crib
Its tongue is ugly and blue

She climbs She climbs
in silence and fury spinning groggy
in darkness and wind Look
her left hand bears for you sweetly
a gift of lightning
and lilies to please you Though

O tonight
in her right hand she she
has invented gravity

...A couple poems here are sort of about stealing other people's stories, which is something I've been teaching my students to do. I know in some classes they call that plagiarism, but not in my class [*laughter*]. We are borrowing, or finding material. Anyway, sorry, I know some of you have heard me read this poem before around Ann Arbor. .....My husband has told me stories about his life. A lot of people I'm close to have told me stories; they feel these are very important stories; and you know, they are right. They become your material. Anyway, this really did happen. My husband tells this story about how he had a salad once that his girlfriend made for him and there was a praying mantis in the lettuce. I thought about that. I feel like I very brilliantly put myself in this scene [*laughter*]. Although it was long, long before I ever met him, it became my story.

Praying Mantis in My Husband's Salad

Once, he found one

among the lettuce leaves and
cabbage shreds a former
girlfriend had

arranged on a plate for him. If

it was still alive, I can't
remember what my husband said that
he and the girlfriend did with it. But
so it is, this

remembrance of the stories of the days of love
with another love of the one you love. She had

blue eyes. He told me that. And
long black hair. She
may or may not have worn glasses. If

she did she would have looked like a scholar in them, and
then the whole sexy scholar thing when she took them off
to lie down beside him on the bed. This

was long before I met him. So
why should I be jealous, or even sad? Even

stranger is
how can I remember it?
And remember it so well?

But I can—having
seen some praying mantises myself.
Their switchblade limbs. The precision
of their folding insectness.

And their Martian faces, of course, with
such innocent expressions.
But all-knowing.
And all business.
And the lettuce-green of them. This

bitch, I looked her up
on the Internet. She's
still alive, in California, where she teaches something
pointless, like linguistics. But

here's the thing: He's never, my
husband, been
a salad-eater. Was he then? Was

the praying mantis he found once in his lettuce
the reason he has eaten
no salad since I met him?

Or was he just in love? Was

he trying to please this salad-tossing girlfriend
from the past, who
offered up to him the last pale-green thing
he'd ever eat again?

Maybe they were brown, her eyes.
Now, I can't remember that, but I'd

bet you any amount of money that her legs were
long, and that she shaved them in his bathtub
with his razor. Her

neck, elegant as a swan's, blah-blah.

But then, imagine

it, their surprise, and just
try not to laugh out loud:

My tiny, triangular head, swiveling
from side to side. My
dead expression, while

my arms (sharpened swords, in fact—for I've
been seen to slice and eat a hummingbird
on National Geographic) seemed

folded up in supplication, or in praise, or in
solemn meditation, just

as they were spreading out their napkins
on their laps, and
raising, perhaps, their glasses in a toast
to the meal she'd made for him, and which
they were about to share, beginning

with that salad, and
also ending there.

This is another retrospective poem, I guess. People ask me a lot of times, you know, when did you start writing poetry? And I say, early, like fifth grade. But I also started tap-dancing in fifth grade. And also I repeatedly won the contests that we would have in gym class for the person who could jump rope the longest without skipping or growing tired. [*laughter*] But none of those things continued along in my life, so it doesn't mean anything that I started writing poetry in fifth grade. But it does mean a lot that it was something that I continued to be encouraged to do once I got here. My parents were extremely practical people. They didn't see the point in me going to college anyway. No one who knew me thought I was college material. But that's all in this poem. So yes, I started writing poetry when I was little, but I came here, and thought maybe I'd be a journalist or something where I was going to make money. I got here and was in the Residential College, and everybody was like, "if that is what you love, it'll all work out," and I would think, how will that work out? I guess I'm lucky I didn't think too hard about it. My family certainly did, asking "What do you think you're going to do with that, Laura?" So anyway, this poem is about that."

> The Time Machine
>
> My mother begged me: *Please, please, study stenography...*
> Without it
> I would have no future, and this
>
> is the future that was lost in time to me
>
> having scoffed at her, refusing
> to learn the only skill I'd ever need, the one
>
> I will associate forever now with loss, with her
> bald head, her wig, a world
> already gone
> by the time we had this argument, while
>
> our walls stayed slathered in its pale green.
> While we
> wore its sweater sets. While we
> giddily picked the pineapple
> off our hams with toothpicks. Now

I'm lost somewhere between
1937
and 1973. My

time machine, blown off course, just
as my mother knew it would be.

Oh, Mama: forget about me.
You don't have to forgive
me, but know this, please:

I am
the Stenographer now.
I am
the Secretary you wanted me to be. I am

the girl who gained the expertise you
knew some day some man would need.

Too late, maybe.
(Evening.)
I'm sick, I think.
You're dead.
I'm weak.

"And now I'm going to tell you
a little secret.
Get your pen and steno-pad, and sit
down across from me."

Ready?
The grieving:

It never ends.

You learn a million
tricks, memorize
the symbols &
practice the techniques

and still you wake up every morning
lost inside your
lost machine. Confused, but always
on a journey.

Disordered.

Cut short.

Still moving.
Keep speaking
Mama.
Please.
I'm taking it down
so quickly, so

quickly, even

(perhaps especially)

when I appear

not to be.

I do this naturally.
See? So

naturally
that in the end

no training was ever needed.

None at all.
None at all.

I taught myself so well.

It's all I can do now.

TUNG-HUI HU

Hopwood Award 1999

Did your Hopwood Award impact your approach to subsequent work?

I received my Hopwood in 1999, a few months before I decided to leave my graduate program for a job opportunity in California. It was a tough decision, but I think the Hopwood gave me enough confidence to leave school, even as it also served as a reminder that I could return to the world of poetry—which I did three years later. I've sometimes thought getting an award is a little like getting a passport: it doesn't necessarily mean that you are smarter or better than anyone else, since these things are always a crapshoot, but it does give you the freedom to move around and experiment more.

Andrea Beauchamp once said that Hopwood winners seem to fall into two groups when they re-read their student manuscripts: pleasantly surprised, or unpleasantly disappointed.

I haven't read the manuscript for a very long time, partly because it's very similar to my first book, *The Book of Motion* (2003). I was admittedly embarrassed by that book for about a decade, as there were poems in there that I had written in college, at the age of 18 or 19; I felt their youth keenly. Now I enjoy that aspect of it: the poems aren't well crafted, but that's perhaps their appeal. Poems don't always end with a great image, as one might expect from a more polished manuscript. And there's some license to go towards indulgence and even cliché in a first book (in using the first person, for example) that one can't really repeat later. While I've moved beyond those poems, I still hear that people like that collection the best—suggesting, perhaps, that it's all downhill after the Hopwoods!

Which poets have influenced your own approach to writing poetry—ranging from "classics" to any contemporaries who may have influenced your mature work? Also, did any so-called "schools" of poetry impress you? Third (and last), are you aware of (or care to share) any non-literary influences that have been especially important to your writing: music, visual art, social change, environmentalism, etc.?

Early on, at the time of my Hopwood award, Charles Simic and his book of prose poems, *The World Doesn't End*, had an enormous impact, as did James Laughlin's "typewriter metric." Now the people are different; I've been trying to (unsuccessfully) imitate Cole Swensen's syntax for years now. There are others, too, that are close to the center of my thinking: Cornelius Eady; C.D. Wright; Evie Shockley; Jena Osman; Bhanu Kapil. And because I've been writing essays recently, writers such as Eula Biss have become important, too. I am sometimes described as a documentary poet, a label which I don't mind, because it means that I count as my peers and colleagues people who share a concern for documenting the social texture of the world around us, its history and its quirks.

The largest non-literary influence in my writing has been film and contemporary art, and I occasionally write reviews or contribute to exhibitions. Much of *Greenhouses, Lighthouses*, is structured as "intertitles" for films, such as Travis Wilkerson's documentary *An Injury to One* or Nagisa Oshima's banned film *Empire of the Senses*; the collection takes on the connections between photography, visuality, and history as one of its key themes.

As I may have mentioned, this is the question I have tried to "personalize" and so my question for you relates to the 2015 interview you did with Rhizome about A Prehistory of the Cloud. Interviewer Jamie Sutcliffe asked you: "... it was interesting to note your tripartite identity as a poet, network engineer, and professor of literature. Could you tell me something about how those identities might be hybridized, and how their inter-relationships might provide interpretative tools for addressing the cloud?" I would like to turn that around just a bit, and ask how their inter-relationships might be providing new expressive, perceptual, and conceptual directions for your poetry. This interests me, in part, because, having studied briefly with Chomsky myself, I am intrigued by your comment: "I studied Chomsky and grammars when learning how to write programming languages in asking how you'd actually parse and understand language."

I should clarify that I'm no longer a network engineer, though I still follow current debates about technology, and occasionally teach electronic literature. Although my own writing remains mostly analog (for now), I think there is a groundswell of interest in digital poetry, because they help us reimagine what "poetry" is outside of the physical page. Poems by authors such as Brian Kim Stefans or Amaranth Borsuk often work as ways of theorizing digital media.

The bigger question is about the sweeping impact that technologies such as the cloud have had on society—and, as I argue in *A Prehistory of the Cloud*, about what the economic models and political fantasies are that sustain those technologies. Language is both a way of reflecting wider societal changes—my undergraduate students use a subtly different argot, even a different syntax—and also a way of representing and therefore shaping that society. Norms around gender pronouns, for example, have changed rapidly in the last few years; as a writer, it's exciting to watch language do something different after centuries of "he" and "she".

As a result, my own poems make their own little efforts to understand what's at the root of those changes; they are arguably technological without necessarily being about technology. In one recent poem, I describe drones through Leviticus's ban on eating unclean birds. In writing it, I was thinking of electronic artist Ricardo Dominguez's observation that migrants at some of the border crossings between California and Mexico have observed a surprising increase in the number of birds—birds, that is, owned by the Department of Homeland Security.

Have you found poetry readings to be useful or enjoyable? Have you been at all attracted to, or intrigued by, the option of sharing poetry (or musings about poetry) online via social media or similar digital venues?

I find poetry readings enjoyable because there's a social dimension to them; I typically read with someone else. Of course, a reading also brings out a different side of poetry for the listener; I've often been told that my poems are a lot funnier when I read them than how they appear on the page, and I learn things about my fellow readers, too. The experience is frequently intimate and there are certain readings that I remember as clearly as any event in my life: for example, that first time I went to the Dodge Festival, standing under a canopy of trees in the New Jersey mud, seeing the poet Ko Un alternating lines with his translator. I'm taking a break from sending out my poems to focus on another book, but poems seem to be primarily read online these days rather than in print journals, so I try to accommodate that.

Do you see modern academia in general as a good professional base for working poets? Do you feel the role of the poet in the academy has had any discernible impact—positive or negative—upon poetry in general?

Poetry often benefits from exposure to other creative and research practices, which the academy offers in spades: maybe it's interviewing subjects (I'm thinking of my students who take ethnography classes); developing translation skills through language and area studies; researching archives of botany manuals or historical letters; thinking about performance in poetry readings and poet's theater; hybridizing creative work with visual work; or getting exposure to some of the political issues that American studies, queer studies, or ethnic studies has called our attention to. I myself took several architecture classes in my second MFA year, and—years later—ended up building a poetry installation in collaboration with an architect.

As a professional base, the academy is good enough to make do, and "good enough" should be the slogan of all resourceful artists. While teaching poetry is orthogonal to my own writing—neither opposed to it nor a direct benefit—I do feel that it keeps me in the game: trying to understand what my students are thinking about and reading keeps me exposed to areas of poetry I wouldn't have access to.

The main worries I have are less about some monolithic "workshop" style that creative writing programs supposedly create than the poor to nonexistent prospects for tenure-track jobs in the academy, and the awful system of adjunct labor that it creates as a result. I think we should spend more time talking about what people do to support themselves as a poet—for instance, someone once told me that Lisa Robertson makes soap, and writes for glossy women's magazines. What we do to write is always more expansive than what most graduate students are told to want in academia.

Here, I'd like to offer you the option of posing a question to yourself that perhaps you've never been asked, or wish you had been asked. Or, perhaps, revisit a question from some past interview that you would now answer differently, or from a changed perspective.

Given that this interview is about Hopwood awards, I'd like to ask myself what I did with the prize money, but I don't remember, unfortunately! I probably saved it for something boring like a security deposit, though I do remember going on a business trip to Arizona around that time—I might have tacked on a side excursion to the Grand Canyon. A colleague told me he spent part of his NEA award on an Xbox, a standard I've always tried to live up to.

* * *

[**Editor's Note**: Brief excerpt from an interview with Tung-Hui Hu by the NEA:]

"**NEA: How does your study of digital media inform your poetry, and vice versa?**

HU: They often circulate around similar ideas. Both my last book of poetry and my interest in the digital cloud—which led to my forthcoming book *A Prehistory of the Cloud*—were sparked by a strange claim of Euripides: the Helen that went to Troy was in fact a fake, made out of clouds. Digital media is similarly cloud-like and ethereal, and we tend to imagine it in the shape of what we as a society most desire."

Source: "Art Talk with NEA Literature Fellow Tung-Hui Hu;" April 23, 2015; by Paulette Beete

DEREK MONG

Hopwood Award: 2005

Luck, Lit, & Gutter Spouts

I was 23-years-old when I won the Hopwood Award for Poetry. A recent college grad, I lived in a leaky apartment that I'd furnished with lawn furniture and posters from old dorms. I read the *Encyclopedia Britannica*—my parents' copy, lugged up from Ohio—when I got bored. I checked email at the library. I blew my laundry quarters on pinball at a nearby arcade. (I hid this fact from everyone I knew.) And then Andrea Beauchamp emailed me. I was at the library. She had good news.

If this sounds like a starving artist's salvation, it's only because I cultivated that image. I never starved because my family had money. I never worried about rent or food or tuition because merit scholarships insured that I'd be fine. If it sounds like the confirmation of young talent, that too would only be half true. I was not a poetic prodigy, even if I believed—as I surely did at the time—that I deserved every sprig of recognition that fluttered my way. What I can say is that I was lucky. I can also say that saying *I was lucky* is often the same as saying *I have means*.

I want to put some words down about luck and privilege and literary awards. I want to do so while outlining just what the Hopwood Awards did for me—aesthetically, professionally—and what they couldn't do, but might have, had I been more mature when I won. I'll start with the latter, which is more interesting, though I don't want to obscure my gratitude to an alma mater and a program that launched me in literature. I owe a lot to Avery Hopwood, whose haunting old portrait in the Hopwood Room still feels like it will burst back to life.

When I won a Hopwood, I still hadn't learned that poems require patience; that the occasional award does not make you flawless; that real success only follows after years of drifting at sea. My Hopwood Award did not help me see this. I thought I had drifted. I thought I'd exerted the labor necessary to shape a poem from the drivel that sloshed around my head. But what qualifies as labor or patience at 23 is admittedly limited, and it would take a few years to see how many years still remained till a book. A big award made my big head bigger; it probably kept me naïve.

My trouble, however, wasn't just age. My trouble stemmed from the fact that I grew up expecting awards. Easy to come by in college, easier in high school, validation blinded me to the real stakes of making art. (I now define those stakes like Stevens: poetry helps the reader live her life.) I'm not sure I understood how big the Hopwoods were. I celebrated by watching *Midnight Cowboy* on VHS with my girlfriend, later my wife. We ate pizza; we drank wine. My life, in short, was going as planned, and I took that for granted. But if it's easy to see your name on an award and accept it as destined, it's hard to see how your path was smoother than most, impossible to some.

This too my Hopwood Award couldn't teach me. It couldn't help me to distinguish—at least not immediately—between two types of luck. The first type travels around literary communities like a sunbeam or rumor, touching this poet or that one. This is the luck that comes when the right poem meets the right judge in just the right mood. This is the luck that comes when a slush pile highlights your talents and downplays your faults. Think of John Ashbery winning the Yale Younger Poets Prize after Auden went *looking* for his book. Think of Edwin Arlington Robinson, whose poems landed, almost by accident, on Theodore Roosevelt's desk. This luck is random.

The other sort of luck looks a lot more like privilege. Think of Robert Lowell, scion of Boston aristocracy, whose very name commanded attention. Elizabeth Bishop called him "the luckiest poet I know!" What she meant, truth be told, was that he was rich. This luck travels through top-tier institutions and influential connections; this is the luck that you cannot luck into or earn. This luck gives you more chances to be first-order lucky in literature (or life). For a long time in poetry, this sort of luck was white, native-born, and male. This luck has parents that care.

I am not Robert Lowell in *so* many ways, but I recognize that I'm lucky in *both* of the ways noted above. When I was a kid, education mattered. My parents bought that *Britannica* and paid for my writing camp. They sent me to Denison University, which propelled me on to a Michigan M.F.A. So I was lucky; I was privileged; I still am today. I was also lucky where other poets—of superior talent or determination—were not. I know because I workshopped with them. I know because I won a Hopwood Award and they didn't. The Hopwood Awards gave me a lot, but not the self-awareness to see how lucky I'd become. That would take years. It would take writing it down.

What my Hopwood Award *did* provide, however, shouldn't go overlooked. First, there's the money. Poetry rarely pays, and when it does the dollars never match the hours we devote to the work. My Hopwood, however, was different, and it remains the most lucrative prize I've ever brought home. I struggle now to remember how I used all that money. A new computer? A little free spending at my favorite bookstore, the now defunct Shaman Drum? Most of it wound up in a bank account, doled out during the months after a teaching gig dried up. By the time we arrived in San Francisco in 2010—five years, six moves, and one wedding later—it was gone.

Then there's the recognition. Is it safe to say that the Hopwoods are the most recognizable prizes for student writing in the nation? I can't think of another that compares. The reason, I suspect, is the esteemed list of recipients that have carried its name: Arthur Miller, Robert Hayden, Frank O'Hara. More recent winners secretly hope—well, at least I do—that a bit of their grandeur rubs off on us. For years I listed "Hopwood Award winner" in my cover letters. I made sure it followed my name in the bios that ran in journals accepting my work. Did this help me publish in additional journals? Perhaps. Did it help me secure fellowships or jobs? I imagine so.

The real value of my Hopwood, however, goes beyond coin or cachet. The real value was the confirmation it provided at a time when I wondered if writing was my thing. I remember the one substantive conversation I had with Richard Tillinghast, just a few weeks into the program—this was just a few months before he left it—where I acknowledged my uncertainty about poetry. Maybe I'd rather take photographs. Maybe I'd rather be a cartoonist. For two years, I told him, I'd give my time to poems, then I'd see where I stood. Richard said that was a reasonable plan.

The Hopwoods helped me commit to poetry. Is this a good thing? There are far worse. Better to commit to poetry, say, than the modern Republican Party. Better to commit to poetry than for-profit healthcare or payday loans. Poetry takes all my free time and frustrates me endlessly, but it can—in its slow, accretive way—change lives. You can draw a direct line, Robert Hass notes, from the Romantic poets to the founding of the National Parks. It runs from Teddy Roosevelt (who read John Muir), to Muir (who read Thoreau), to Thoreau (who read the Romantics.) And this, *voila*, proves Shelley right: poets are the unacknowledged legislators of the world. Emma Lazarus's "The New Colossus" still gives voice to the humane (i.e. non-Republican) take on immigration.

I'm incredibly grateful then that poetry is part of my professional life and that the Hopwoods helped that happen—psychologically, professionally, and financially. Still, luck played a role. Two years ago, I won that national lottery, conducted each fall, wherein hundreds of qualified poets vie for 20-30 tenure-track teaching jobs. My luck didn't just snag me a paycheck; it offered stability. I now own a home and—long after my peers in business or law—other big kid toys like a retirement plan, warranties, and gutter spouts. Poetry bought my gutter spouts. Poetry pays for my childcare. Poetry, in the end, secured me more time to write poetry, which feels, let's be honest, uncharacteristic of poetry. (Poetry's relationship to the poet is mostly vampiric, rarely transfusive.) It is unsettling to admit this, but by the standards of my rural neighbors, poetry made me rich.

It may come as no surprise then that I celebrate the poet's infiltration of the academy, even as I wish there were more spaces in academia for poets. (Again: why should *I* be so lucky?) Education offers poets a rare chance to stay connected with their art while paying the bills. It also offers them, if they're wise enough to take it, the chance to read laterally *and* historically. This is something I didn't learn during my M.F.A., though I was steeped in it during my doctoral work. I am a professor of creative writing *and* American Literature, as delighted to discuss Frank Bidart's linebreaks as Phillis Wheatley's subversiveness. The academy taught me that. I now teach it to others. And as a teacher, I see more clearly the good that the Hopwood Awards can accomplish. Many of my undergraduate writers are first generation college students. Some are students of color. The beauty of the Hopwood Awards is not what they can do for me, but what they will do for writers who look nothing like me. I'm thinking of my students. I'm thinking of what it would mean for them to receive a letter from their Representative—mine came from the wonderful John Dingell—congratulating them on their Hopwood Award.

I'm thinking how that's an award that I want attached to my name.

POETS AT MICHIGAN: THE MIDDLE YEARS

[Transcribed excerpt from the video] [29]

Cody Walker
Panel Introduction:

Hi, I'm Cody Walker, from the Department of English. Welcome to "The Middle Years." I may be the right person to introduce this panel if only because I am in my middle years, or perhaps even my middle year. On birthdays, Tom Lynch always tells his friends to "go for the 100," and, well, I turned fifty a couple of months ago. So: right in the middle.

The way we're defining the Middle Years here, though, is somewhat less precise. It's a rather thick middle—beginning with Theodore Roethke, who did undergraduate and then graduate work at U of M in the late 1920s and early 1930s, just a handful of years after Frost's final stint as a poet in residence. The early 1940s brought us Robert Hayden, who was pursuing a Masters degree, and W. H. Auden, who was teaching a famously impossible-to-get-through syllabus and smoking a lot of cigarettes. Frank O'Hara was here in the early 1950s, and Marge Piercy just after that. Donald Hall joined the English Department faculty in 1957 and stayed 18 years, leaving in 1975 with an Ann Arbor native, and a great poet, Jane Kenyon. X. J. Kennedy worked on a Ph.D. here in the late 1950s and early 1960s, winning two Hopwood Awards along the way. And I want to pause right there, because X. J. Kennedy, or Joe Kennedy, to his friends, is I think one of the great

---

[29] "Poets at Michigan, Then and Now— The Middle Years." Introduction by Cody Walker. Panelists: Laurence Goldstein, John Knott, and Thomas Lynch. University of Michigan College of Literature, Science, and the Arts. (May 1, 2017). Available at: https://www.youtube.com/watch?v=Z1OddIGT5Oc&t=546s

living American poets, and also one of the great comic spirits of our time. He's 88 and still enormously energetic – he published a very funny novel a few years ago, he published a new collection of poetry only a month ago, and he enthusiastically agreed to be on this panel when we invited him several months ago. Unfortunately, his wife Dorothy, who was also a grad student at Michigan—the two met in an Austin Warren seminar and were married in Ann Arbor—has taken ill, and Joe needs to be by her side. So I'd like to suggest that we raise a glass to Joe and to Dorothy, and to wish them all the best wishes that can be wished.

Back briefly to the narrative. In 1969, Robert Hayden returned to U of M, this time as a professor, and stayed until his death in 1980. Nobel Laureates Czeslaw Milosz and Joseph Brodsky taught here off and on in the 1970s and 80s; MacArthur Award winner Alice Fulton taught here in the 1980s and 90s.

So that takes us up to the turn of the century, and to the end of our thick middle. For a more comprehensive tour of Poets at Michigan, you can go to the Hatcher Grad Library, in the lobby space just off the Diag, and see an exhibit that tells the story from Frost to the present. You can see Frost's letters, Roethke's doodles, and O'Hara's Hopwood poems. It runs until the end of the month. And now it's my great pleasure to introduce our panelists.

Laurence Goldstein is Professor of English at the University of Michigan and the former editor of the university's flagship scholarly and creative writing journal, *Michigan Quarterly Review*. He's the author of four volumes of poetry, including the breathtakingly brilliant *A Room in California*, and the author, editor, or co-editor of many scholarly books, most recently *Writing Ann Arbor: A Literary Anthology*. His most recent work of literary criticism is *Poetry Los Angeles: Reading the Essential Poems of the City*. Larry is also one of the co-organizers of this symposium, and he's in many ways the institutional memory of this place – the person I go to when I have a question along the lines of "What was Robert Hayden like?" Larry is wise, and funny, and generous – and he's also retiring in about two weeks. This may be his last public address before becoming an emeritus professor. It's hard for me to imagine the English Department without Larry – and I hope that I won't have to. Maybe you'll come visit us twice a week? Three times a week? Anyway, when we don't see you, we'll assume that you're busy writing, and we'll look forward to the books to come.

John Knott joined the Department of English of the University of Michigan in 1967. He published three scholarly books on Renaissance literature in the 1970s and 1980s; in the 1990s his teaching and research interests gradually shifted to literature and the environment. He published a critical book that grew out of a course he developed in the literature of the American wilderness, *Imagining Wild America*, and has edited or co-edited several collections dealing with the environment, including *The Huron River: Voices from the Watershed* and *Michigan: Our Land, Our Water, Our Heritage*. John was Chair of the Department of English from 1982-87, during which time he started the MFA program in creative writing. He also helped establish the Institute for the Humanities and the Program in the Environment, and served as director of each, before retiring in 2006. When we found ourselves short one panelist a mere two weeks ago, the committee immediately thought of John – and he quickly agreed to join us. Thank you, John, for that kindness – and for your fifty years of service to this community.

Thomas Lynch is the author of five collections of poems, four books of essays, and a collection of stories. And I may not even have the math right; Tom has written a lot of books. His work has been the subject of two film documentaries, the first of which won an Emmy and the second of which won The Michigan Prize awarded by Michael Moore. He's taught with the Department of Mortuary Science at Wayne State University, with the graduate program in writing at the

University of Michigan, and with the Candler School of Theology at Emory University. He's a charter member of the faculty of the Bear River Writers' Conference, where he's a much-beloved workshop leader in basically any genre: poetry, fiction, memoir, you name it. He lives in Milford, Michigan, where he's been the funeral director since 1974, and in County Clare, Ireland, where he keeps an ancestral cottage. That's a bio line I'm always a bit jealous of. It makes Tom sound like a figure from a fairy tale. And there is something both larger than life and impish about Tom. You want to be around him to see where his imagination leads, and you want to be around him to hear his laughter. My students have been reading from his collection, *Still Life in Milford*, these past couple of weeks, so they've already experienced how he masterfully balances gravity and levity. Now you'll get to as well.

I give you Larry Goldstein, John Knott, and Tom Lynch.

Laurence Goldstein
Thank you. This second panel is charged with speaking about poets who, as students or faculty spent time at the University of Michigan from the date of Robert Frost's residence in the early 1920's through about 1990. This is an impossible task. But we will try to stimulate your interest in the range of wonderful poets who have settled here for a short or a long period. I'd like to begin by reading a poem about Ann Arbor written by a University of Michigan undergraduate in the early 1950's: Anne Stevenson, who is now one of Great Britain's most honored poets. Her collected poems was published by Oxford University Press in 1996. The poem, titled "Ann Arbor *(A Profile),*" appears in her first volume, *Living in America,* published by Generation Press thanks to funding by the Board of Student Publications funded by the University of Michigan. Though the author has published a revised version of the poem in *The Collected Poems*, the earlier version offers some perspectives on its subject closer to the sensibility of a very

young poet. See if you can spot any differences between the Ann Arbor of the 1950's and the present day.

Ann Arbor *(A Profile)*

Neither city nor town,
even its location is ambiguous.
Of North and East and Middlewest it both is
and is not; in every case,
a hopeless candidate for the picturesque.

Trees and a few grand old
accidentally preserved houses
save it from total suburbanization,
give it the mildly authentic complexion
of secondhand furniture.

No setting for tragedy,
It is the scene, nonetheless, for more
than its surfeit of traffic would suggest.
Entrances and exits are frequent enough
to be anonymous; every year
the young adolesce in its residences;

the usual academic antipathies
enliven the cocktail parties,
while, driven from their garrets,
dim graduate students gripe in the beer joints,
leaving their wives to cope with babies
and contemporary interior decoration.

In all the tongues of the world
its tone is Germanic and provincial.
Yugoslavs, Hindus, Japanese

fraternize in the supermarkets
where bean sprouts and braunschweiger
are equally available.

Love is frequently experienced
over jugs of California claret.
Politics are important,
and culture so cheap and convenient
that any evening you can expect thin strains of Mozart
to issue from half a dozen windows.

The women who do not run for alderman,
paint pictures, write poetry or give expensive parties
for the members of visiting symphony orchestras.
Their children are well-fed, rude and intelligent,
while alone in immense mysterious houses live the witches
who remember the coaches of the first city fathers.

A microcosm, something of a mosaic,
always paradoxical, with scenery it has little to do.
And if you venerate antiquity or feel wiser
where there is history, you will, of course,
prefer Cambridge,
though even there, the proportion of good people
to bad architecture is probably about the same.

As we heard this morning, Robert Frost's residence at the University of Michigan is the perfect example of the mutually beneficial cooperation of academia and the literary world. President Marion Burton wanted to enhance the art community on campus. To do so, he turned to one of the most celebrated authors in the country. The previous panel has reminded us how complex and fruitful the negotiation can become between writer and administrator and how rewarding the outcome can be, resonating down to our heartfelt tributes of gratitude today. Robert Frost was the perfect choice; the right person at the right time. If we think of the literary situation a generation earlier, we have to ask whether poetic geniuses like Walt Whitman, Emily Dickinson, Edwin Arlington Robinson, and James Weldon Johnson would have fit so smoothly into the classrooms of the university in the early 1920's. They would certainly have shaken up the English Department and the students, and that might have been a very good thing. But as inspiring oracle and a wily rule-breaker, Frost was an excellent choice to begin the tradition of seeking and signing up of an eminent writer to meet with students and guide them through their first literary efforts.

What we learned also is that it takes a strong-minded University President and College Deans to enact that kind of radical change in teaching protocols. I would cite the kindred example of nearby Olivet College as well. In the late 1930's, President Joseph Brewer decided he wanted to make the College more arts-friendly. He established a summer writers conference, and when Ford Madox Ford showed up, he buttonholed this British man of letters and offered him a job. Ford, the author and co-author of 32 novels and many books of literary history, was a great novelist. The word "great" has become problematic in our time, but I cling to the definition I first heard from a professor of mine at UCLA: "A great poet is someone who has written at least one great poem." I would specify Ford's *The Good Soldier* as a great novel. Robert Frost inspired his students by compelling them to study and recite great poems of the past. Ford Madox Ford undoubtedly told many anecdotes about the great authors he had personally tutored and helped to become eminent: Joseph Conrad, D. H. Lawrence, Virginia Woolf, Henry James, and Ezra Pound among them. Those were fortunate students.

We know that in the 1920's and especially in the hungry decade of the 1930's the poetic tradition was honored in the academy. But living poets, some of them very hungry indeed, were kept at arm's length.

Faculty committees often resisted the notion of hiring poets. There was a palpable fear of having the center of literary study bend too far to the modern and contemporary. Students might prefer, in numbers too large for comfort, to enroll in poetry writing courses rather than in poetry study courses. The visiting poet, always a *he* rather than a *she*, seemed to be an acceptable compromise for both the institution and the poet. The school would see its reputation enhanced and the poet could finance his next couple of years of creative solitude as he began or finished a new poem or new poems.

In the twenty years that followed Frost's presence in the English Department, only two poets of his stature graced the University. Theodore Roethke, born and raised in Saginaw, received a BA here in 1929 and an MA in 1936. Roethke was an unruly, and in some ways, unstable student, but clearly, from his first year at U of M, a genius. When I arrived here in 1970, Roethke's freshman composition teacher, Carlton Wells, was still on the faculty. I asked him about Roethke, and he said his clearest memory of him was that in a course that required weekly compositions, Roethke never turned in any work until the last day of the semester, when he dumped some sixteen short essays on Wells' desk and exited hurriedly from the classroom. Roethke hoped to join the faculty here, but a nervous breakdown in the 1930's followed by a spell at Mercywood, a local hospital, discouraged the University—alas — from placing him on the faculty.

Also in the 1930's we find universities confronting the Great Depression as well as the oncoming war in the European and Pacific theaters. Some exiles from Europe found their way to shelter in America, such as the Frankfurt school of cultural critique. That would be, among others, Teodor Adorno, Max Horkheimer, and Herbert Marcuse, as well as composers like Arnold Schoenberg and Igor Stravinsky, filmmakers like Fritz Lang and Jean Renoir, playwrights like Bertolt Brecht, and authors like Christopher Isherwood and W. H.

Auden. These immigrants contributed significantly to the modernist design of American culture and we are still profoundly in their debt.

W. H. Auden taught a summer school course at the aforementioned Olivet College in 1941, and then began teaching at the University of Michigan. In 1940, Auden's volume, *Another Time*, had conclusively demonstrated that this 33-year-old prodigy was a major poet. Almost every poem of his we study in anthologies is a work of the 1930s. Like Frost, his exalted reputation drew our English Department into its glorious spotlight and put us on the map of great institutions welcoming to poets and poetry. As it happens, Auden refused to teach either creative writing or modern poetry, though he was ever-watchful and nurturing for young poets who showed the same spark of early talent he possessed in his undergraduate years.

Thirty years after he left Ann Arbor, Auden worked with the U of M administration to bring Joseph Brodsky to the Slavic Languages Department. In 1987, when Brodsky was no longer in residence here, *alas* again!, he was awarded the Nobel Prize for Literature, and in 1991 he was appointed Poet Laureate of the United States. One of the student poets who most impressed Auden was Robert Hayden, about whom I would like to speak at more length. Like Roethke, Hayden was Michigan-born and bred. He grew up in Detroit, an industrial powerhouse associated, of course, with the automobile—the single greatest symbol of American leadership in manufacturing. I'm sure I am not the only person to see a dynamic connection between Detroit and Ann Arbor; seemingly so unlike, as Anne Stevenson suggested, but linked by their shared respect for intellect in advanced technics. Robert Hayden's earliest verse, so far uncollected, focused on the figures of workers in the automobile factories, just as Diego Rivera did when painting his magnificent murals at the Detroit Institute of Arts, the iconic heart of Detroit culture. Like Auden and Frost, Hayden addressed matters of historical concern; specifically, African-American experience. Hayden's Hopwood Award-winning manuscript, *The Black*

Spear, has poems of sweetness and light, but also poems about black history in America full of anger and resentment. He wrote so-called proletarian poetry about life during the Depression, and especially the hard life of dwellers in the Detroit ghetto where he grew up.

Auden could see that this was a poet on his way to greatness, and the two authors kept in touch for the rest of their lives. Hayden received a Bachelors Degree from Detroit City College, now known as Wayne State University, in 1942, and a Masters Degree from the University of Michigan in 1944. When in the mid-1940's and shortly after he began writing masterful poems like "Frederick Douglass," "Those Winter Sundays," "The Ballad of Nat Turner," and "Middle Passage," he dared to hope that he might be taken on as Assistant Professor by the University that knew him so well, but that was not to be, and he took a job at Fisk University in Nashville in 1946. Overworked, he nevertheless wrote one superior poem after another. We can credit Russell Fraser, duly appointed Chair of the English Department, for journeying to Fisk in the late 1960s and offering Hayden a position here as Full Professor. Hayden was not the first person of color to teach in the Department; that would be Lemuel Johnson, an émigré from Sierra Leone, who was hired in 1967. Johnson's three volumes of poetry, which he named the *Sierra Leone Trilogy*, focused on West African history. Using an experimental style, he opened up historical materials of which almost every American remains ignorant.

Few modern poets have seen more deeply than Robert Hayden into the historical depravity of human beings. But amazingly, few poets have been a more persuasive ambassador for the uplifting vision of humanity so essential to our lives. In her study of Biblical literature, *For the Love of God*, Alicia Ostriker writes these words: "How to praise is one great lesson of the Psalms. Literature in English is irrigated by these poems. Not only because of the multitude of memorable phrases in the King James version, but also because they are always telling us to celebrate, praise, open ourselves to the universe. That is the task of a poet, or at least I take it to be my task as a poet and human being, attempting to open myself in praise of an existence that inevitably includes suffering anguish, pain, despair."

The hiring of poets to teach our students, the institutional support for activities like the Hopwood Program, and the Hopwood Room, the encouragement of all student writing at the undergraduate and graduate level; (not just poetry), that nourishes the public imagination, subventions for the University of Michigan Press with its enormously influential series, *Poets on Poetry* as well *Under Discussion* as scholarly treatments of poems and poetics—these are services of the House of Intellect. I have to add I saw this morning in the list of Guggenheim Fellowship winners, the name of Victoria Chang who was in a creative writing class I taught, and who has now just published her fourth book. Onward Victoria!

Language amplifies our sense of the real, as many poets and scholars have labored to explain. Support given by educational institutions to this super-pleasurable super-civilizing activity is an empowering of what is hope-inducing in our literate society. I'm sorry to repeat myself, but this truth cannot be too often repeated, especially in these dark times. Robert Hayden succeeds in speaking of beauty in the human and natural world. Like Frost, Roethke, and Auden, and like the Afro-Jamaican poet Lorna Goodison, and African-American Thylias Moss who joined the Michigan faculty in the later decades of the 20th century, he believed with all his heart in the public benefit of a poetry that enhanced the quality of life for its readers. It is appropriate that Hayden was named as the Poet-Laureate of the United States by his fellow Michigander, President Gerald Ford. The present poet laureate, Juan Philipe Herrera, has pledged to carry forward Hayden's humanistic vision.

Always in speaking of one poet, we pay tribute to other poets who carry on the same inspirational work. I want to close by speaking briefly of two poets who performed this redemptive task for students in the vast stretch of years under discussion: Donald Hall and Jane Kenyon. Donald Hall taught for some twenty years in the Department of English in this university, from 1957 to 1977, the longest period of any major poet. That is how I see him; as major, as eminent, and canonical; a superb technician, and through his books of poetry and poetry criticism, immensely influential on poets from the 1950's to the present. He, too, served as Poet-Laureate of the United States. Like Roethke, Hall and also his student, and later his wife, Jane Kenyon, wrote with an inspired voice of praise that Alicia Ostriker refers to as psalm-like; joyful in the abundance of flowers and birds and fields and forests and the changing seasons. And he is brutally honest in his appraisal of the social condition in the post-modern period. Both poets travelled the country bringing their poems to appreciative audiences. Not long after their marriage, they moved to New Hampshire, but retained contact with friends and fellow-poets in Ann Arbor. Jane Kenyon's evocations of the New Hampshire rural landscape, and of her own personal sorrows, have had a profound effect on young poets in America and abroad. The love poems of this exquisitely-matched couple are just what the Biblical psalms mandated, not to mention the Song of Songs. And Don's grief-stricken poems after Jane's death respond to and extend Theodore Roethke's famous elegy for his student, Jane, "thrown by a horse." How much we have all learned about joy and sorrow having taken the poems of these University of Michigan authors to heart.

Many poets have passed through the hallways and offices of this campus. I think of my predecessor as Editor of *Michigan Quarterly Review*, Radcliffe Squires, whose *Selected Poems* will be published by Wake Forest University's Library Partners Press this year. And Nancy Willard, Radcliffe's favorite student, a Newberry-Award winner who delighted so many—probably millions—of readers with her books of poetry for children and teenagers, and her many volumes directed at adults. You don't have to be an English major to write distinguished poetry. The University of Michigan continues to provide a temporary home for creative writers, and they repay their host by making this a genuine art city; a utopian site of envy and gratitude for readers around the world. Let the parade continue.

A more extensive discussion of the topic "Poets at the University of Michigan, 1925-1980," can be found in a special issue of *Michigan Quarterly Review*, Winter 2018, edited by Keith Taylor.

John Knott [excerpt]
Lee Bollinger's Presidency which was 1996 to 2002 was a time when the arts received extraordinary support from the highest levels of the administration. He found the considerable funds necessary to bring the Royal Shakespeare Company to Ann Arbor for the first of what turned into several residencies, and made it possible for the English Department to bring a number of high-profile writers to campus for readings, including Derek Walcott and Seamus Heaney—both after they had won the Nobel Prize…..

Lee's active patronage of the arts was unusual but not unique. Harold Shapiro, who preceded him, raised the money that made it possible to launch the Humanities Institute, and spoke at its inaugural event: a reading by [Hopwood Award winner] Arthur Miller from his own biography, *Time Bends*, after hosting a dinner for Miller and his wife….he was a great fan of Miller's plays, a genuine fan. Other administrators responded to opportunities presented by the faculty, and one that I remember, that Larry has mentioned, was bringing in Joseph Brodsky, or at least making it possible for him to teach here. He came, really, as some other dissidents did, because of Karl Proffer's presence here in the Slavic Department. And the fact that he and his wife ran a publishing house, Artis, which was a mecca for dissidents in those days. Brodksy left for a year…and then came back here for six more years….

One thing I've noticed from my flirtations with administration here is that, I think writers have going for them—including poets—is a glamour that administrators at the college or the university level don't typically associate with demographers, physicists, [etc]...good writers can command attention outside the academic community as well as enliven the community itself, and at Michigan at least, the people who control the funds have often responded to the ability of poets to appeal through their poems to the broader public...

Today's lively writing scene at the University—and it is very lively with its large contingent of writers and regular and visiting faculty appointments...may seem normal to our students. But if they had arrived in 1967, as I did, they would have found a very different scene. Allen Seeger, the only bona fide fiction writer in the English Department at the time, had just retired. We were better represented in poetry with Radcliffe Squires and Donald Hall and, by 1969, Robert Hayden as well...They were all estimable poets, but not so much a community of writers as a collection of individuals with respective distinctive spheres of influence.

Donald Hall would leave in 1975 with Jane Kenyon to see if he could make it as a free-lance writer living on his grandparents' New Hampshire farm.....In his time at Michigan, Donald Hall was a charismatic teacher who could draw a hundred non-English majors to a lecture course designed to introduce them to poetry. He brought attention to the University through his reputation and his extensive friendships with prominent poets...Many of these came to Ann Arbor to give readings at a time—the 60's and early 70's—when poetry readings were still a relatively new phenomenon on college campuses. Visitors in those days, including all friends of Don's, included Robert Bly, Galway Kinnell, James Wright, Adrienne Rich, Philip Levine, and Gary Snyder, among others.

For a while, Bert Hornback, a fourth colleague, ran a series of weekly readings with minimal funding, and later, in the early 1980's, organized a spectacular evening of poetry in Rackham Auditorium with an all-star lineup. Maybe some of you were there. He charged $5.50 a ticket to cover the cost of renting the auditorium and getting the poets here; all friends who welcomed the chance to spend time with each other The program....consisted of serial readings by Donald Hall, Galway Kinnell, Wendell Berry,...it was a lollapalooza of a poetry reading, to a full house, plus standing room (ticketed standing room; the auditorium holds 1,100), with scalpers selling tickets on the steps of Rackham Auditorium....Donald has written about it in his memoir, *Unpacking the Boxes*.....

Despite this burst of activity, there was relatively little funding for bringing writers to campus apart from that of the Hopwood Program for the annual reading in the winter and the lecture in the Spring—both associated with award ceremonies.

The existence of the Hopwood Room was crucial to the English Department's decision to launch an MFA Program in Creative Writing in the early 1980's, a program that would metamorphose into today's Zell Writers Program. That and the support of faculty who thought we should expand our commitment to creative writing...and who were willing to do the work necessary...most prominently Larry Goldstein and Jack Aldridge, who was then directing the Hopwood Room. The tradition of support for creative writing at Michigan that the Program represents...made it easier to win the necessary approvals to offer a new degree. We knew that we would have to cobble together funding necessary to attract students, and assumed (rightly, as it turned out) that they would win their share or more of regular Hopwood awards. I was Chair of the English Department at the time and organized two receptions for past Hopwood winners, one in New York and one in Ann Arbor, to renew their connection to the University at a time when we were placing greater emphasis on creative writing and also to jumpstart fundraising....Arthur Miller spoke at the New York reception along with fiction writer Max Apple and screenwriter David Newman. They represented three generations, and Miller testified to the importance of his undergraduate experience at Michigan; he was always willing to do that, and he subsequently made a generous gift....A number of out-of-towners came to the Ann Arbor event.

One of them was John Ciardi; in his prime known as a poet and translator, the editor of *The Saturday Review*, a TV and radio personality, and for a number of years, I am told, after WWII, he was simply the most popular poet in the country—the best-known. Like Miller and others, he was drawn to Michigan by the reputation of the Hopwood Awards. Ciardi told me he had borrowed money from his Uncle Max for his tuition, and when Uncle Max asked how he would pay him back, Ciardi said he was going to win a Hopwood Award—and he did.

Our young MFA Program became the English Department's primary vehicle for bringing in visiting writers with whatever funding we could put together. When Nick Delbanco came to Michigan to take over the Directorship of the program…he steadily raised its profile, making it one of the best in the country. Among other things, Nick created new opportunities for students to interact with visiting writers, by instituting residencies for almost a week for selected visitors. They would give a reading and perhaps another presentation, participate in classes, and meet individually with students....And we had learned that MFA students wanted fresh perspectives on literature courses. Writing faculty who joined us in the 1980's and early 1990's included poet Richard Tillinghast [and] Alice Fulton...."

Thomas Lynch [excerpt]
This is a delight and a pleasure. When I first got word of this event and my invitation to it, I was very grateful that it was taking place in National Poetry Month, because it gives me an opportunity to remind us that one of the things we should do in National Poetry Month is to

buy poetry at retail, and that man in the back from Literati Booksellers has proof positive that poetry is being committed in Ann Arbor and its environs by people you may be sitting with, and if you buy a book of poetry you can re-gift it to that brother-in-law who seems to have everything—but he doesn't have any of *those*, I promise you....You can learn a lot of things hanging around with poets and writers and the rest, but in particular it puts me in mind of the Russian Joseph Brodsky. The year that he was hired to come here—I think he was the second Poet in Residence after Frost, and he was basically hired not to teach people how to write poems, but just because he was to walk around and be a sort of fixture in the imaginative life of the students in the way that Frost was. In the year that he was invited to do that, in 1972, I was recently enrolled in (and was president of the class, by default) of what would become the 1973 class of Mortuary Science at Wayne State University. So that in the fullness of time when, after publishing a poem some years later, I could be known as a "Poet-Funeral Director." That's sort of a hyphenated life I know the publicists have tried to make a lot of; I guess like a cop who becomes an opera star, or a wrestler becomes a governor, or a performance artist who becomes President.

The idea to me is that in this particular time, it is very important that the precision of language—in this age when the systematic top-down abuse of adjectives has become rampant—it is important that we are careful about this language. I say this because, though I want to talk a lot about Joseph Brodsky and William Butler Yeats, I'm not a scholar as are the fellows that I'm with today. I was at that reading, John, by Wendell Berry and Seamus Heaney, and I was watching the scalping of tickets, and came home saying to my wife, "What a wonderful thing that people are paying for poetry.".... So I think these are times when precision in language is very, very important. So days like today, ...and books like the ones that are being peddled in the back there, are extremely important. My wife Mary often says to me that a poet-undertaker is like a proctologist with a sideline in root canals: people don't really want that stuff. But I can tell you that if you buy a book of poetry in Poetry Month, and tell your adult children or grandchildren that you attended a poetry reading today, they will fear you in ways they don't currently—I promise. Just try it.

I was at a conference in Galway some years ago, and I had the good luck of launching a book that year at this particular conference. The star of the show for the conference that lasted a full week was Seamus Heaney. He was reading poems when he came to a poem he called "Audenesque." It was based on the notion that Auden had when he got word of Yeats' death in 1939—January 28th—he commenced writing "In Memory of W. B. Yeats;" a poem that appeared, I think, in that book…published in 1940. So from death to elegy to the book's publication took a year, which is lightning speed by my lights. And in that poem, you will recall (I think it's the last section) where Auden, who I always imagined was on his way to Michigan at the time he wrote this….where he had a job lined up for the following year. "Earth, receive an honored guest; / William Yeats is laid to rest. / Let the Irish vessel lie / Emptied of its poetry."

He was—and Heaney was quick to point this out—he was trying to commune with the dead in this act of elegy. Art, actually poetry, is what we do, according to Auden, to break bread with the dead. And Heaney added, when he was introducing his elegy for Joseph Brodsky, that, if art is what we do to break bread with the dead then rhyme and meter are the table manners, and that actually, in writing "Earth, receive an honored guest; / William Yeats is laid to rest…." Auden was mimicking Yeats' late rhyme: "Irish poets, learn your trade / Sing whatever is well-made…." …That was written, I think, in late 1938…I'm thinking November; I'm thinking he knew he had days that were numbered. But in honoring the dead man that early 1939, Auden's effort was to mimic not only his honor and affection for the man, but to mimic his table manners. Not only to break bread, but to break them in the same rhyme and meter that he'd been given by the Irish master.

So that when Heaney wanted to honor Joseph Brodsky, who died, as it turned out strangely, on January 28th, the same date as Yeats almost 60 years later (1996, I think it was); was he 55? Too young. Was it New York? Was it like Yeats, dying in a foreign country? Who's to know. But to Joseph, Heaney wrote:

> Joseph, yes, you know the beat.
> Wystan Auden's metric feet
> Marched to it, unstressed and stressed,
> Laying William Yeats to rest.
>
> Therefore, Joseph, on this day,
> Yeats's anniversary,
> (Double-crossed and death-marched date,
> January twenty-eight),
>
> Its measured ways I tread again
> Quatrain by constrained quatrain,
> Meting grief and reason out
> As you said a poem ought.
>
> Trochee, trochee, falling: thus
> Grief and metre order us.
> Repetition is the rule,
> Spins on lines we learnt at school.

I thought, sitting there in the theater in Galway, what a great thing to have this conversation, ongoing, amongst and between poets, who down the decades and centuries and generations, seem to pick up where the other ones left off. [....]

Interview with Donald Beagle, Editor:
Radcliffe Squires: Selected Poems 1950-1985 Centennial Edition

[Interviewed by Frances J. Pearce, the author of *Those Carolina Parakeets Once Far from Extinct* (Finishing Line Press). Her poetry has been published or is forthcoming in *My South* (Rutledge Hill Press), *Archive: South Carolina Poetry Since 2005* (Ninety-Six Press), *Kakalak*, *Fall Lines*, and *NCLR Online*. She is the immediate past president of the Poetry Society of South Carolina, the oldest state poetry society in America.]

While attending graduate school at the University of Michigan, you had the opportunity to do an independent study with Radcliffe Squires. How did that come about and what was Squires like as a teacher?

The University of Michigan is unique for its Hopwood Writing Awards—an endowment that funds annual student creative writing competitions. And some early Hopwood Award winners, like playwright Arthur Miller, have endowed complementary awards over the decades. In my time on campus, most contest entries came from English majors, of course. Because I was in the graduate Library Studies / Information Science program, I went to the Hopwood Room to see if I could enter. To qualify, I was told I first had to submit a collection of my student poems to one of UM's resident faculty poets. If any agreed to endorse me for an independent study, I could become eligible. Donald Hall had left for New Hampshire only a short time earlier. But even had Hall stayed in Ann Arbor, I strongly suspect Radcliffe would still have been my preferred choice. I had read Hall's poetry at length and was, of course, duly impressed. But I had heard Squires read at a bookstore reading in Ann Arbor in 1971, and was, quite frankly, dumbstruck. His stylistics and metaphysics both marked him to me as something of a maverick, perhaps even an outlier, whereas Hall's work seemed to me to epitomize the mainstream of excellent contemporary poetry. And let me emphasize that I agreed with that assessment then, and still do. Hall's work fully deserves the accolades it has always received, and doubtless will always continue to receive. But I knew I needed to find my personal inspiration elsewhere.

I went to Hatcher Library and poured over books by Squires. I was fascinated to find that Squires took remarkable risks, constantly tested limits, and pushed the envelope in ways that made each succeeding collection a creative leap from its predecessor. But then, on my arrival in Ann Arbor, I also learned that he'd been on leave for months in the aftermath of his wife's tragic and untimely death, so nobody knew if he was ready or willing to take on any independent study students. Fortunately, Squires did read and approve my submitted manuscript. I was once told (but have no way to verify) that I was his only student that Fall of 1976. I can verify that he liked my work enough to give me an A+ at the end of Fall Term. A scrap of urban legend (relayed to me by my graduate faculty advisor) once held that I was the only graduate student to ever receive an A+ from Squires for an independent study. I am very skeptical of that rumor, but it did do wonders for my grad school GPA. My formal independent study with Radcliffe ended with Fall Term 1976, but through his own generosity, he then volunteered to extend it informally ("off the books" as he described it) through Spring 1977. He actually spent a good deal of time that Spring away from Ann Arbor, so our meetings were far less frequent, but longer in duration. Still, it was a rewarding extension, because that Spring term culminated in milestones for each of us. He received and accepted the invitation to give his historic reading at the Library of Congress for its Archive of Recorded Poetry and Literature (April 18, 1977), and then came the announcement that my student collection had won the top award in the "major poetry" category of the Hopwood Awards.

What criteria did you use in selecting poems to include in the Squires edition?

The preceding death of Radcliffe's wife, Eileen, had two clear influences on our interactions as professor and student, especially in the more formal Fall 1976 term. It caused me to carefully steer clear of any questions about his personal life—that felt like walking on eggshells. But at the same time, that personal loss seemed to motivate him into a period of deep self-reflection about his own writing, to the point that he seemed willing to discuss the body of his own work published up to that time. So I followed his lead and tried to be a good listener. Along with our extended discussions about my own student poems, I interspersed queries about which of his poems were favorites, and which might be best candidates for later anthologies or cumulative editions. He was not inclined to discuss his first collection, *Cornar* (1940). And at first, he seemed guarded about his second book, *Where the Compass Spins* (1951). But the third and fourth collections, *Fingers of Hermes* (1965) and *The Light Under Islands* (1967) were clearly open to discussion. I was keeping a personal journal in those years, which I have preserved, so those old lists (informed by my current editorial judgment) were helpful in selecting titles from those collections. Added selections came by way of three additional poems requested by Theodore (Ted) Haddin, who wrote the wonderful Afterword for this new book, with the encouragement of Dana Gioia. Like me, Ted had been a student poet under Squires, but Ted's study came decades earlier, while Radcliffe and Eileen were newly established in Ann Arbor in the 1950's. Ted's experience was very different than my own in Fall Term 1976, when Radcliffe's mood had turned understandably dark, and he evidenced a world-weary pessimism for a time. But then early Spring 77 brought the Library of Congress invitation, which brightened his mood and outlook considerably, and he suddenly became willing to discuss his most recently-published book, *Waiting in the Bone* (1973). He also finally opened up more about *Where the Compass Spins*. Later that Spring, Squires also discussed some of his newest poetry still in progress, which included several of the "garden" poems that he read at the Library of Congress on April 18th, and that also later appeared in his extraordinary 1981 book, *Gardens of the World*. Selecting poems from these last two books was challenging because nearly every poem in the 1981 collection (published by LSU Press) is superb. I never discussed the seventh collection, *Journeys*, with Radcliffe to any degree, even though our correspondence extended to 1988 (he died in 1993). Here I must tip my hat to eminent poet Dana Gioia for not only recognizing the extraordinary quality of Squires' work as a whole, but also for so expertly shepherding Radcliffe's final collection, *Journeys*, into publication in 1983.

Did you have any difficulties in obtaining permissions from original publishers?

Yes, publishing currently operates under a framework of intellectual property law that makes permissions a potential minefield. All the people I dealt with were friendly and collegial. The problem is that we are all caught up in a maddeningly muddled copyright environment. One of Squires' publishers (LSU Press) notified me that they were already negotiating with a vendor-aggregator to digitize their entire out-of-print backfile into an e-book database, including their Squires title, *Gardens of the World*. This rang alarms because, as an academic library director, I knew that meant if I delayed too long making decisions about editorship, selection, or sequencing, my entire project could suddenly be derailed by corollary and arbitrary restrictions imposed by this third-party e-book aggregator, whose priorities lay with packaging and marketing their database, not with the literary merits of any individual title. This made it *essential* that this book be published in calendar year 2017, or there might not be another window of opportunity *within our lifetimes*—quite literally. Persons unfamiliar with leading-edge issues of digital library development may not appreciate the urgency of this point—and that is understandable. But any academic library director who has tried to negotiate with publishers such as Elsevier will understand my sense of urgency.

The University of Michigan Press did not present any such digitization dilemma, fortunately, but their approval process was tightly-structured and shaped the format of my entire book. Their contract stipulated that I insert a header page identifying the source collection, as realized in my header: "Poems from *Fingers of Hermes* (1965)", and then immediately follow that page with all the poems selected from that book. Then I had to do the same for "Poems from *The Light Under Islands* (1967)". No other publisher imposed such format specificity. But this UMich Press requirement obviously shaped the layout of my entire edition; I could hardly use one format for poems from those two books, and then switch to some other format for the rest. I also kept the order of poems from those two books *exactly* the same as their original order in the UMich Press collections. I did, however, take the liberty of departing from this rule elsewhere. My selections from *Where the Compass Spins* fall in a slightly different sequence from their order in Squires' original book, simply because I want the reader who starts on page one to enter the body of Radcliffe's life-work in a certain thematic context. And the order of choices from the fifth and sixth collections was complicated by the fact that quite a number of poems from *Waiting in the Bone* (1973) were republished in *Gardens of the World* (1981). So I decided to lead with three poems that appeared only in *Waiting...*, followed by poems that had appeared in both collections, followed in turn by the extraordinary series of "garden" poems that had only appeared in the later LSU Press collection. Even more fundamentally, however, permissions issues dictated my role as solo editor-of-record, causing me to abandon my original notion of doing this book as a potential collaboration or co-editorship. And permissions issues also impacted my decision to publish this with Library Partners Press @ ZSR Library / Wake Forest University (LP Press for short). Not only had LP Press (under Director William Kane) done exemplary work publishing my own recent poetry collection, *What Must Arise: Poems* (January 2017), but their status as an academic imprint put out by the Library of a major university (roughly following the model of Stanford University Library's HighWire Press) provided me the added protection of asserting the "Academic Fair Use" doctrine should any controversies arise over copyright surrounding the book's release. An example emerged with Squires' poem "Letter to an American," which originally appeared in *The New Republic* (1957). A revised version of this poem later appeared under a different title ("Epistle to W. M.") in

Fingers of Hermes. This was not one of the poems Squires had shortlisted in our 1976 conversation, but I very much wanted to discuss it, with quoted excerpts, in my Editor's Introduction, because it speaks to the themes of Squires' social consciousness and environmental awareness. I discovered that *The New Republic* now subcontracts out its permission requests to a legal consultancy firm, and that firm's approval regimen is both Byzantine and expensive. But it was a simple matter for me to notify them that I was limiting the extent of my excerpt from "Letter to an American," and surrounding it with interpretive analysis that should qualify my use of that excerpt at no cost under Academic Fair Use. In its reply, the firm only requested confirmation that my book was indeed being published under a provably academic imprint. Upon receiving details about Library Partners Press they quickly relented and agreed to my assertion of Academic Fair Use. This spared me possible *months* of negotiations, and prohibitive expense, over a single poem. This alone validated my decision to avoid any non-academic publisher, though the Academic Fair Use doctrine also proved crucial to my use of a few other poems (such as "Pasture Fever.").

Which Squires poems have been anthologized most frequently?

One obvious answer would be "The Envoy," because it first appeared in the 1983 anthologized portfolio of poems from major American poets titled *Northern Lights*, issued by Palaemon Press, and then, after its interim republication in *Iowa Review*, again resurfaced in the 1996 anthology *Hard Choices: An Iowa Review Reader*. But here is my key point: in the 1960's, Radcliffe's poetry was beginning to draw the sort of major critical attention and favorable reviews that, in prior decades, would have likely moved his best poems into any number of major anthologies. But the mid-1960's also saw the beginnings of a fierce balkanization of American poetry and criticism, resulting in fragmentation of the anthology market. My favorite example is the 1969 anthology, *Quickly Aging Here*. It hit bookstores in 69-70 with a buzz of "experimentalism" that continued through the start of my college undergraduate career. In a sense, it (and similar anthologies of that time) sucked much of the oxygen out of the room for middle-aged academic poets like Squires who were rooted in quasi-traditional forms, but who were also testing limits and pushing the envelope in ways that stayed true to the notion that the aesthetics of poetry remain important. This debate is still going on today. In a 2016 review in the *Times Literary Supplement*, Edith Hall, a classics professor at King's College London, wrote that modern "…critical theory [such as] New Historicism and poststructuralism, has consistently evaded aesthetics. It has scant language in which to discuss the motivations of many people who enjoy poems, art galleries or musical performances: that they find them beautiful."[30]

Even though *Quickly Aging Here* did contain some arguably good poems, as a whole it marked yet another retreat from any discernible criterion of aesthetic beauty. True, that ferment of the late 1960's through early 1970's had upsides; it allowed some previously marginalized poets to suddenly gain attention. But it also tended to marginalize a number of poets like Squires, whose work was just on the verge of gaining the attention it had long deserved.

But let me return to that question of aesthetics. Modern life confronts us with much ugliness. Surely our poets should feel empowered to confront and interpret such topics, but must their poems be inherently ugly to do so? A fair example would be Squires' poem, "Extinct Lions"—an example of his poetry drawing upon ecological concerns. The extinction of any animal species—in this case, a subspecies called the "Barbary Lion"—is an inherently ugly topic. Yet, I find "Extinct Lions" to be an extraordinarily beautiful poem. The poem's image of

---

[30] Quoted in: Eric Adler, "When Humanists Undermine the Humanities." *Chronicle of Higher Education.* May 14, 2017. Available at: http://www.chronicle.com/article/When-Humanists-Undermine-the/240067

the lion's face as a "golden web" in a dream-like realm of Jungian collective memory actually intensifies the tragic magnitude of this animal's extinction. One might say this poem's inherent beauty never compromises the integrity of its underlying ethical expression. Therein we find a certain paradoxical sophistication that, in my view, too often escaped the superficial editorial and marketing impulses that motivated a number of anthologists of the 1960's and 70's.

What are the major themes in Squires' poetry?

Several years after his death, the UM English Department posted a memorial webpage (still online) that includes this quote from Squires: "My major themes involve a belief that we have gotten too far out of Nature, we humans, ever to be able to think of it as home again."[31]

I've always felt some pre-20th century romantic-era poets had begun to sense the seriousness of humanity's estrangement from nature, and responded (somewhat indirectly) by trekking into the European Alps in search of "the sublime." Squires turned that strategy on its head. His poems about his horseback rides into alpine landscapes and his journeys into the deserts of his native American southwest were never written to escape or evade our estrangement from nature. Instead, he uses those expeditions to emphasize that alienation; to confront and articulate its almost inevitable (and possibly fatal) consequences. Similarly, his elegant explorations of classicism through Greek and Roman history and mythologies do not evade the crises of our contemporary world, but rather transform those goddesses and gods into dramatis personae that return to personify the perilous realities of our time. Two quick examples: "A Letter to Pausanias" follows in the footsteps of that noble Roman geographer who once explored the

---

[31] Quoted in: "Memorial: James Radcliffe Squires 1917-1993," *Faculty History Project: University of Michigan*. Available at:
https://www.lib.umich.edu/faculty-history/faculty/james-radcliffe-squires/memorial

ruins of the Greeks who'd lived before his own era. Squires' poem does indeed rediscover the ruins of a Greek temple once described by Pausanias. But around that temple, the poem then further describes the intrusive trenching of a 20th century archaeologist (also abandoned), and then beyond all that, perched on a peak above the temple, the poem describes a metal radar tower installed as part of an atomic attack early-warning system. The poem thus quite brilliantly juxtaposes these divergent time-frames by way of their artifacts—religious temple, scientific trench, and military tower —into a sort of super-positioned temporal collage that straddles the centuries. Finally, Squires' great sequence of garden poems includes "The Garden of Prometheus," who was of course the mythic figure punished for stealing fire from sky gods and giving it to humanity. Squires morphs Prometheus into a melting glacier (an "ice-giant") and thereby creates, in 1977, one of the earliest literary expressions about the danger of climate change and the start of the great glacial melt.

In what way did Squires' critical work influence his own poetry writing?

Squires' motivation to write his important studies of Allen Tate, Robinson Jeffers, and Robert Frost did, in my mind, very closely relate to their respective influences on his own poetry. To keep this brief, Tate's struggles to re-interpret the legacy of the "old south," as in his "Ode to the Confederate Dead," while also interrogating their veneer of antebellum and Confederate mythology, helped Squires find new ways to integrate his own fascination with the far-more-distant antiquity of the classical world and its own attendant mythologies with his modernist sensibility. Jeffers, in turn, blazed poetic trails into the unique psychologies and geographies of the American west in ways that helped Squires revisit the stunning backcountry vistas of his own native Utah and the high country of Wyoming with fresh perspectives. Frost presents a more complex example. As Squires wrote on p. 17 of *The Major Themes of Robert Frost*, "…it is difficult to sound anything like Frost without sounding too much [like Frost]…" So Frost's influence was less stylistically obvious, yet, in some substantive respects, ran even deeper. For example, Squires' discussion of "West-Running Brook" (approx. pp. 99-103 of *The Major Themes of Robert Frost*) ventures quite beyond the normal regime of literary criticism. Squires instead delves into a fascinating comparison of the poem's metaphysical underpinnings with an essay by William James that explores scientific questions of entropy and thermodynamics. Radcliffe discovers that James used imagery that anticipated Frost's poem to a surprising degree. The point I would make (also made in my Editor's Introduction) is that Squires' poetry similarly engages certain frontiers of modern science to an unexpected degree—from the early relativistic imagery of "The Subway Bridge" through the cosmological musings of his mid-life "Rapture of the Deep," and finally to his deft late-career asides in the "Journeys" sequence that hint at a number of enigmas related to quantum theory. I'm sure Squires would have made such excursions even had he not studied Frost. But I think his critical exploration of Frost's deceptively disguised metaphysics helped Squires find his own individualistic ways to infuse imagery from scientific research into his poetic imagination.

Why isn't Radcliffe Squires more widely recognized today?

I think the best response to that question might be found in the closing paragraph of Anne Stevenson's wonderful review of the *Selected Poems* edition: "After a gap of over fifty years, returning to the poetry of a Radcliffe Squires I hardly knew and of whose importance (even to my own development) I was certainly not aware, I am surprised by how contemporaneous his work seems, and yet how passionate, how daring, how imaginatively ambitious *as art* it is, compared to most poetry served up today in the service of 'social consciousness and environmental awareness'. Squires completed his study of *The Major Themes of Robert Frost*, in the 1960s, when his more 'feral' affinities were acknowledged in another critical tribute, *The Loyalties of Robinson Jeffers*. Yet Squires himself, as profound and original as either of these influential figures, has somehow been allowed to slip out of the American canon. Should we attribute his neglect to the egalitarian present's downgrading (and loss) of poetry as a special, or in Steven's terms, a 'noble' art? Or is it more likely that Squires was simply ahead of his time? What serious young poet in 2018 could fail to see what Robert Frost and Robinson Jeffers saw in respect to nature, and before them, William Wordsworth (indeed!), and what Donald Beagle saw when he reissued Squires' poetry and I saw when I rediscovered it? That is, without throwing away or despising the imagery of mythology and religion, the poetic imagination must expand into the vast wonderland and frightening reality of contemporary science. It is impossible to imagine poetry continuing to be a serious art in the future without this global and universal dimension."[32]

---

[32] Anne Stevenson, "Radcliffe Squires: Poet of Real Deserts and Imaginary Gardens." *The Dark Horse*. Spring & Summer 2018. p. 89.

Made in the USA
Columbia, SC
23 December 2018